Richard Spencer

May 2014.

Divide and Ruin

The West's Imperial Strategy in an Age of Crisis

LIBERATION MEDIA

SAN FRANCISCO

Written by

Dan Glazebrook

Staff

Saul Kanowitz, Keith Pavlik

Liberation Media

2969 Mission Street #201

San Francisco, CA 94110

(415) 821-6171

books@LiberationMedia.org

www.LiberationMedia.org

Divide and Ruin

Divide and Ruin

The West's Imperial Strategy in an Age of Crisis

Introduction

THINGS were not looking good for imperialism in 2008. The occupations of Iraq and Afghanistan, so loudly trumpeted as "victories" a few years earlier, were suffering increasingly heavy blows at the hands of dogged resistance movements, and economic crisis had broken out across the entire Western world. Huge chunks of the globe appeared to be breaking free from decades of subservience to U.S. and European domination, with popular leftist movements coming to power throughout Latin America, and Colonel Gaddafi's vision of an independent and anti-colonial African Union was gaining currency across the continent. U.S. weakness was underlined by a disastrous attempt to use Georgia as a stalking horse against Russia in a highly symbolic failure of Western military might to impose its will. Everywhere, it seemed, the neocolonial grip of the U.S. and Europe was being forced loose.

On an ideological level, imperialism had been exposed as never before. The Iraq war turned what used to be treated as conspiracy theory—the notion that Western governments were prepared to slaughter hundreds of thousands of innocent people in unprovoked acts of aggression to further their imperial interests—into incontrovertible common knowledge. Meanwhile, the anti-globalisation movement—and even its establishment counterpart, the Make Poverty History campaign—had alerted the Western public to the reality of debt extortion and the role of international finance in the perpetuation of third-world poverty and hunger. No one could claim to be ignorant of the mechanisms by which the rich world kept the poor world poor anymore.

Many of us at the time felt that the game was up for the Empire. Of course, the U.S. and European ruling class was never going to simply give up its global dominance without a fight—and history shows that it is precisely when they are *losing* power that ruling elites are at their most brutal. But surely, it seemed, their aggression would from now on be exposed and isolated. The idea that just three years later, leftists, liberals and Muslims the world over would be cheerleading the bombing of yet another Arab country by the very countries that had destroyed Iraq, and would be doing so with apparent UN and Arab League support, seemed unthinkable.

> *The truth is that Empire's strategy today is far more insidious than in the days of Bush and Blair.*

The truth is that Empire's strategy today is far more insidious than in the days of Bush and Blair. Imperialism today no longer swaggers onto the world stage in a cowboy hat declaring its determination to launch "crusades" on behalf of the "haves and the have mores", to use the memorable phraseology of George W. Bush; its strategy today is a lot more cunning. Its new wars are not, in the main, fought by white people in U.S. and European uniform, but by bearded jihadi militants (as in Libya and Syria) or black African armies (as in Mali), commanded by an "anti-war" politician—of African heritage—who came to power by posing as the very antithesis of Bush. At the same time, imperialism's new wars are sold as responses to crises—the cry that "something must be done" to prevent genocide in Benghazi or Damascus seeming a lot more urgent than Bush and Blair's cack-handed attempts to craft justifications for wars to which everybody knew they were already committed.

This move to a reliance on proxy forces rather than imperialist troops, however, is not only an attempt to bewilder and confuse. It is also driven by the reality of military and economic crisis. The estimated $3 trilllion cost of the occupations of Iraq and Afghanistan, the domestic political difficulties resulting from tens of thousands of dead and disabled soldiers, and the inescapable fact of military defeat, mean that direct conquest and occupation is no longer a viable option. The shift to war by proxy is thus also a sign of vulnerability and weakness.

At the same time, economic and military crisis has led to a reduced ambition on the part of the imperial states. As the late historian Eric Hobsbawm put it when I interviewed him in 2008, "[The

U.S.] can still destroy us all, but it cannot make the world go its way any more". The wars in Afghanistan and Iraq have demonstrated this clearly. The new governments in both countries, despite being the products of outright conquest by imperialism, often refuse to toe the line of their Western patrons, with Afghan President Karzai frequently denouncing U.S. operations and recently signing a mineral rights deal with China, for example, and the Iraqis refusing to support Western foreign policy on Syria. The puppetmaster cannot even control his own puppets.

This is the natural result of Empire's declining economic influence. It cannot compete with the very generous terms of trade offered by China, and is thus at risk of losing all its contracts in the third world. For Western imperialism, today more than ever, strong independent third-world states are seen as a dangerous threat, because all are viewed as potential economic partners of China.

Of course, during the Cold War, this was also true—every independent third world state was a potential Soviet ally. But at least anti-communist strongmen could be relied on to pick the U.S. as a partner rather than the USSR. The U.S. could ultimately "outbid" its Soviet rivals for the allegiance of third world states. This is what has changed. Backing the U.S. and the West is increasingly a game of diminishing returns.

The West realizes this, and understanding that any genuinely independent strong state is unlikely to do its bidding anymore, prefers to see such states destroyed. It is only in this context that we can understand the apparently ludicrous policies pursued by the West across the Middle East: the promotion of vicious sectarianism, the banning of major political parties, barring former officials from work and so on. These policies are not designed to produce stable, compliant states, as in the past, because the West has realised that in its crisis phase such things are no longer possible. They are designed to produce weak, divided "failed states", unable to become regional powers in their own right, and unable to become powerful allies of China or anyone else. Thus, the much-criticised "failure to plan" in Iraq, was a plan in itself.

This book tracks the emergence of both these developments— the move to proxy war, and the move to destroy, rather than control, potential regional powers. Neither are new, of course—the British

Empire was largely built by proxy forces, and attempts to destroy regional powers—and prevent their re-emergence—are as old as colonialism itself. It could even perhaps be argued that it was the existence of the Soviet Union that forced a move away from this strategy as imperialism was forced to support strong states governed by anti-communist generals in order to crush the emergence of popular anti-colonial movements likely to ally with the USSR. The current strategy could thus be seen as a "reversion to type" after a period of unwilling adjustment to the reality of a serious global challenge, coinciding with a similar "reversion to type" of capitalism itself, falling back into its natural crisis-mode after a historically brief period of successfully postponing or exporting the impact of its inherent contradictions.

Although this book is a collection of articles which were written as individual pieces over an extended period of time, I hope I have chosen and arranged them in a way that works as a (more or less!) coherent whole. Part one addresses the current crisis, both its economic and its military aspects, illustrating the unfolding disaster of military occupation, not only for the native populations (never a concern for imperial planners), but also for the legitimacy of the belligerent states, both abroad and domestically, including amongst their own armies. Part two looks at the overall strategic imperialist response to this deepening crisis, whilst part three develops the analysis by looking at how Empire has sought to manipulate events in Libya, Mali and Egypt to prevent the emergence of a unified and developed African bloc able to resist subordination to Western institutions. Parts four and five look in more depth at the intricacies of imperialist war strategy in Libya and Syria, and part six examines some elements of the media presentation of these conflicts, both through news reporting and through the entertainment industry. Finally, part seven examines the impact of imperialism's crisis strategy on oppressed communities in Britain, and the unrest this has generated in response.

Feedback and dialogue is always welcome; please feel free to make contact via the email address below.

Dan Glazebrook,
Oxford, April 2013
Danglazebrook2000@yahoo.co.uk

Part One
Imperialism in Crisis

Back to the natural state of stagnation

*A review of 'The Great Financial Crisis:
Causes and Consequences' by John Bellamy Foster
and Fred Magdoff (Monthly Review Press)*

Originally published in the Morning Star, 12 August 2009

ONE of the few boom industries in a time of slump, it seems—aside from private security firms, debt collection agencies, and locksmiths—is the publishing of books about slumps. Everyone from Vince Cable to Channel 4 News editor Paul Mason is touring the country touting their own take on recent economic events, and copies of Das Kapital are reportedly flying off the shelves faster than they can be printed. What makes this short book, by the editors of the long-standing U.S. left journal Monthly Review, stand out is that it looks beyond the shenanigans of high finance to the deeper, structural causes of capitalism's current malaise.

Fifty years ago, Paul Baran and Paul Sweezy published their classic work on political economy in the latest phase of capitalism: Monopoly Capital. In it, they argued that mainstream economic thinking on recession was topsy-turvy from its very inception. Whilst mainstream economics tended to ask why the Great Depression occurred—thereby implicitly accepting that it was some kind of freak occurrence—Baran and Sweezy argued that it was in fact capitalism's *growth* periods that required explanation. Capitalism in its monopoly phase—the age of the giant corporation—is *characterised* by stagnation, and only experiences anything different due to historically-specific—and temporary—"fixes". At the root of this stagnation lies the ultimate contradiction of capitalism—that productive capacity tends to outstrip effective demand; that is to say, the buying power of the international working class necessarily falls short of what is necessary to purchase all that it produces. To put it simply: we are not paid enough to buy all the crap we produce. The result: Goods pile up unsold, productive activity freezes up, and capital is unable to find avenues for profitable re-investment. This is standard for monopoly capitalism, and the Great Depression in this sense was just the return to normal conditions.

The Second World War provided the ultimate "fix" to this problem—the wiping out of large amounts of capital, paving the way for a new round of investment. This led to the "Golden Age" of capitalism, which lasted until the late 1960s. Eventually, however, the system reverted to its natural state—stagnation. Foster and Bellamy's argument is that, since then, the main (attempted) fix has been the *financialisation* of the economy. Denied profitable investment opportunities in the "real world economy" of production of goods and services, capital has instead flowed into finance—into a series of increasingly volatile and over-inflated asset price bubbles—most recently the real estate bubble. For a time, this was a double boon for capital—not only did mortgage lending provide an extremely profitable outlet for surplus profits (so long as house prices kept rising), but rising equity on people's houses also allowed them to refinance their homes and take out ever larger consumer loans. These loans became the driving force of the U.S. economy, since real wages have been in decline for the majority for more than three decades. Credit became the new "fix" to that classic problem—if people cannot afford to buy all the crap they produce, well then we can *lend* them the money to do so!

It was clearly a "solution" built on the most fragile of foundations—and Foster and Magdoff predicted precisely the nature of the crash well over a year before it occurred.

What made Baran and Sweezy's "stagnation thesis" radical at the time, was that capitalism was still in the throes of a twenty-year boom—a "Golden Age" of unprecedented growth—and therefore did not *look* particularly stagnant. Today, however, reality confirms its validity everywhere you look. The challenge for the left is to articulate both the temporary nature of capitalism's fixes *and of capitalism itself* in terms accessible to all—and this book is a useful weapon for all who strive to do so. □

A review of the Oxford Literary Festival 2010

'They actually quite enjoy it': The senseless futility of the Afghan war

Originally published in the Morning Star, 29 March 2010

NO less than four of the lectures and discussions on the opening weekend of the Oxford Literary Festival focused on the Afghan war. Yet the attendance at all of them could barely have been sparser. Whilst the political and military establishment grow increasingly worried about the war and its unwelcome consequences for the projection of Western power, the public have seemingly grown desensitised to the unending casualty reports that have now become the staple diet of news reports and the obligatory introduction to every Prime Minister's Question Time. The war has become normalised, its senseless brutality and pointlessness an accepted backdrop to the surreal spectacle of British politics.

Nothing illustrates this more clearly than the opening night panel discussion, "Afghanistan: Why are we there and when will it end?" It soon becomes clear that this is not so much a genuine question for the panellists to answer as a rhetorical cry of despair. Of course, some passing attempts at explaining the continuing military presence are put forward. Bruce Anderson talks of the need to "deny a failed state to our enemies", alluding to the supposed terror attacks that withdrawal would provoke. He says this even after Tory MP and ex-officer Patrick Mercer has already rubbished such a view earlier in the same meeting, claiming that "Anyone who tells you that the Afghan war is about keeping the streets of Britain safe is more stupid than they look". Mercer argues instead that we need the army there as part of a *regional* war, one extending from Iran to Russia. He doesn't elaborate on this thesis, but presumably the idea is that bombing Afghan villages will somehow serve to intimidate Putin and Ahmedinejad. Revealingly, over all four of the sessions, no one any longer even attempts to seriously defend the assertion that the Afghan war is about securing civil liberties and women's rights for the Afghans.

Helmand's mammoth poppy crop is mentioned—but, as Sam Kiley noted, "It was definitely not part of British strategy to hit the opium trade" when they entered the province in 2006. Indeed, the portion of drug profits that accrues to the Taliban, even in the areas under their control, are "chickenfeed" according to Kiley. They receive a tax on the poppy crop, but the bulk of the profits, he claims, are made by ISI—the Pakistani secret service. Other big players in the trade include the Helmand police chief and President Karzai's brother. In other words, drug profits mainly accrue to the allies, not the enemies, of the British military presence—and these profits are, in fact, greatly *inflated* by this troop presence, which puts the price up and makes other business impossible. No surprise, then, that despite a comprehensive crackdown on Al-Qaeda's financial structures, the West has not attempted anything similar with the financial structures of the Afghan heroin trade.

Some explanations are closer to the mark. For Bruce Anderson, to leave would be a "tremendous blow to Western prestige and to Western strategic interests". For Sam Kiley, withdrawal would empower Islamists and "would reveal vulnerabilities" within NATO. What these arguments really boil down to is that we're there because we're there and we need to win because we cannot be seen to lose. We need to reinforce our strategic "credibility" by winning wars. This is power for it's own sake; senseless and hopeless. This is clearly seen in the blasé response given by Bruce Anderson to a question about Afghan civilians. Apparently, the thing about Afghans is that they are a tough and hardy race, you see, so "they don't mind taking a few casualties"; in fact, "they actually quite enjoy it".

As for when this nightmare will end, the speakers were all of one voice: no time soon. "Whilst you may question the reasons for going in, there is no debate that now we are there, we cannot simply pull out", explains Bruce Anderson, to the accompaniment of vigorous head-nodding from the rest of the panel. It is an argument we have heard many times before; one which attempts to stifle political debate under a cloak of supposed moral obligation. It is also, of course, an argument that could equally apply to any act of aggression you might care to mention; after all, was Poland not suffering under a brutal military dictatorship before the Nazis tried to liberate them in 1939? Did the Wehrmacht, too, by Anderson's logic, not also have a moral obligation to stay "until the job was done"?

Jaunty young officer Patrick Hennessey called for a bit of "strategic patience", and pointed out that the war in Northern Ireland lasted for 30 years. When I suggested that the lesson of Northern Ireland was surely that there *are no military solutions* to such conflicts, and that political negotiation is the way to peace, Tory MP Patrick Mercer replied that the British had gone too soft on Ireland, and should never have laid down their weapons. In other words, the Good Friday Agreement was a bad idea and it would have been much better to have continued the war. That was not an answer I was expecting. As Bruce Anderson put it, the difference between Ireland and Afghanistan is that, in Ireland, "The bad guys decided they couldn't win". Quite so, Bruce. But who were the bad guys in Ireland exactly? And how long will it take them to realise they have no more chance in Afghanistan than they had there? □

Arab resistance and the end of US hegemony

Originally published in a one-off journal Palestine and U.S. Hegemony by Sons of Malcolm, 9 July 2009

U.S. hegemony is over. The Project for a New American Century—the blueprint for global military domination cooked up by Cheney's mob—is in tatters less than a decade into that century. On the economic front, the "neoliberal" model of unregulated markets—which allowed U.S. companies to extort billions from the third world during the 1990s—is now universally ridiculed. A new global order is emerging. South America—seen by the U.S. as their "backyard" for almost 200 years—is finally breaking free of neo-colonial rule and electing independent and anti-imperialist governments in one country after another, most recently in El Salvador. The Middle East has seen anti-imperialist parties steadily gaining in strength, notably in Palestine and Lebanon. Meetings of the World Trade Organisation in recent years have ended with Western governments unable to dictate policy to the countries of the global South in the traditional manner—an unprecedented victory for the people of the world.

How has this about turn come about, when only ten years ago, the U.S. was the world's policeman, seemingly able to impose its will anywhere it chose?

On the one hand, the rise of China has been crucial. No longer does the threat of U.S. sanctions on a third-world country carry with it the fear of famine and isolation. Chinese markets can easily accommodate those goods the U.S. will not buy. Over the past ten years, most countries in the global South, especially in Africa and Latin America, have massively increased their exports to China, and this has left them much less vulnerable to U.S. economic pressure.

But any student of history will tell you that the single most common factor in bringing about large-scale change is military defeat.

U.S. military-economic power never fully recovered from the blow it received in Vietnam. For the best part of a decade, U.S. military operations were effectively driven underground, relying on proxies such as the Contras in Nicaragua to do the U.S.'s bidding rather than using the U.S. army itself. In the 1980s, Reagan declared that the Vietnam syndrome was over, and sent U.S. forces into Lebanon and Grenada; but the world's biggest truck bombing sharply curtailed the Lebanon adventure, and triumphing over tiny Grenada was hardly an awe-inspiring feat. What really gave U.S. firepower a much-needed shot in the arm was the gratuitous self-destruction of the USSR at the end of the decade. Imperial powers have always followed up slave rebellions with the murder of thousands, mostly unconnected with the initial revolt; and so it was that the defeat of the USSR—nothing more than a 73-year slave rebellion in the eyes of U.S. planners—was celebrated with the crucifixion of Iraq. The highway of death saw 80,000 retreating soldiers and their families massacred, and sanctions would ensure that the country remained a dysfunctional and grisly reminder of the price of disobedience to the New World Order. Millions perished from the malnutrition and medieval diseases that swept the country in the wake of the attack, which had destroyed almost the entire infrastructure of the country—including electricity, water and sewage systems.

Most third-world leaders absorbed the intended lesson, and reacted accordingly. The International Monetary Fund used its new-found monopoly on loan provision (heralded by the collapse of the USSR) to turn the screw on the South. The 1990s were the era of the Structural Adjustment Programme—massive public spending cuts that decimated public services and industries and forced millions into poverty. It was no coincidence that this enforced slashing of health and education budgets was accompanied by an unprecedented surge in the AIDS epidemic across the developing world.

Not all countries followed suit. Yugoslavia refused to play ball, and paid the price in 1999 when subjected to a 78-day blitzkrieg at the hands of NATO forces. It was not the total success that has often been made out. NATO did not manage to force onto Milosevic the deal he rejected—that their soldiers be allowed "free and unimpeded access" to the whole of Yugo-slavia—but instead signed up to what *he* had offered *them* before the bombings—autonomy for Kosovo. Yugoslavia's will had not been broken by the use of overwhelming force and the U.S. had failed to achieve its aims—but this fact and its implications were lost amidst the triumphalism. Events two years later, however, would make the point in a way no one could ignore.

The events of 11 September 2001 showed that even an arsenal as big as the rest of the world's put

The Palestinian people heroically resist occupation despite Israel's overwhelming military superiority.

together could not prevent the sole superpower from being humbled. It shattered the U.S. myth of invincibility and invulnerability, and showed that foreign adventures would have consequences from which no one was immune.

For Cheney's boys in The Project for a New American Century, however, it was the moment they had been waiting for to put their plan into action—a chance to project U.S. power right up against the old Soviet borders in Afghanistan, and even into the oilfields of Iraq if the gullibility of President and public allowed. So it was that the U.S. army, with Blair and other carpetbaggers hanging on their coattails, entered what Saddam Hussein predicted, correctly, would be the graveyard of U.S. imperialism. In hindsight, very few will now publicly accept that this was a good idea. The common analysis now is that—in the case of Iraq at least—this war was unwinnable and should never have been started. This analysis, whilst perhaps actually true, nevertheless misses a fundamental point: The war might have been won. The U.S. had amassed the world's biggest arsenal at the same time as Iraq had been systematically destroying its own capabilities at the behest of the UN. What prevented a U.S. victory was a determined, dogged popular resistance movement on the ground. It is precisely this resistance that has kept the U.S. army tied up and bogged down in ever-extended tours of duty, thus paving the way for leaders such as Chavez in Venezuela and Morales in Bolivia to carve out independent paths for their countries without risking the U.S. invasions that would have been the inevitable corollary of their policies in an earlier era.

And the resistance has not been limited to Iraq and Afghanistan. Palestine has been the crucible of Middle Eastern anti-imperialist resistance since at least 1948. The failure of Israel to eliminate either Hamas or Hezbollah has emboldened the Iraqis, as well as Iran, and has shaken U.S. stooges such as Mubarak in Egypt—who correctly fear the emergence or strengthening of similar anti-imperialist grassroots resistance movements in their own countries. Israel's 2006 invasion of Lebanon was intended to be a dress rehearsal for a U.S.-Israeli attack on Iran. The ability of Hezbollah to force Israel into a retreat without having met their war aims put paid to those plans.

Let us consider where we might be had the Iraqis, Palestinians and Lebanese given up their struggle and accepted defeat. The PNAC may well have spread by now to Iran, Syria, perhaps even Korea or Cuba—presumably under the leadership of John McCain, Sarah Palin and Tony Blair. There would have been no soul-searching critiques or regrets or inquiries in the mainstream political arena. It is despair in defeat, not shame in guilt, which has prompted the flood of MPs claiming they were misled and lied to. And yet, as things stand, the greatest military superpower stands impotent. They still wield vast destructive power, but to what end? They can still shock—but they can no longer awe. ☐

Part Two
Imperialist Strategy in an Age of Crisis

Privatisation and bombing

Two sides of
the same coin

---

*Originally published as a leaflet for the Occupy demonstration in Bath,
10 November 2011*

THE PROBLEM IS NOT LACK OF MONEY

According to the Sunday Times "Rich List", the 1000 wealthiest individuals in Britain increased their wealth by £60 billion between May 2010 and April 2011. This is not on the back of economic growth; the economy, as we all know only too well, has been stagnant. Therefore, this money has come *directly* from other sections of society; a redistribution of wealth from the working- and middle-classes to the very richest (75% of British people saw their real incomes decline in the same time period). Warren Buffet, the world's third richest man, put it very clearly: "It's class warfare. But it's my class, the rich class, that's making war. And we're winning."

Three years ago, the banks were bailed out with public money, to the tune of hundreds of billions of pounds. We are now told that we need to lose the bulk of our hard-won public services in order to pay off the huge debt this bailout incurred. Cameron said "frontline services" would not be affected, but this was a lie, as is now becoming more and more obvious. Bristol Council has already announced plans to close ten of its twelve residential nursing homes, and to abolish homecare services for the elderly completely. Even the NHS, who Cameron told us would be exempt from cuts, has now been told to find £20billion "efficiency savings".

We are often told that there is "no alternative" to public spending cuts, because we need to "reduce the deficit". This is nonsense. The total private wealth in Britain amounts to £9000 billion (£9 trillion). Just under half of this—£4 trillion—is owned by the richest

10% of the population. A *one-off* wealth tax of just 20%, to be paid only by the richest 10%, would pay off the entire national debt of the country (£800 billion) in one go. A Yougov poll commissioned by the Glasgow Media Group found that 74% of the British population supported this idea. But this alternative does not even get an airing anywhere in the mainstream media. Instead, we are told that public spending cuts are the only solution, despite the fact that they will not only cause misery and unemployment to millions, but will not even begin to pay off the national debt, and will in fact plunge the economy into an even deeper recession.

> *A one-off wealth tax of just 20%, to be paid only by the richest 10%, would pay off the entire national debt of the country...*

So why is the establishment (all three mainstream parties and the entire media circus) so committed to this path, and so deaf to the calls to do something to challenge the power of the banks? In a word, because they are all owned by the banks (in the case of the media) or sponsored by them (in the case of the politicians), either directly or indirectly. They rely on them for election campaign donations and for advertising income. They will not bite the hand that feeds them. But they do not feed us; they rob *us*—and we most definitely *should* be biting their hand.

THE PROBLEM IS TOO MUCH CAPITAL

So why do the banks want the government to close down all our public services? The big problem for the banks at the moment is that they have more money than they know what to do with. If money cannot be profitably invested, it loses its value. But in a recession, there are very few places to profitably invest. They are nervous of investing in the housing market, because another big crash is looming. There is no point investing in manufacturing (e.g. the car industry etc), because markets are already glutted- there are already too many products that cannot be sold. This is where public spending cuts come in. Cameron says he expects the private sector to step in where the public sector gets cuts back. Put into plain English, this means you will increasingly have to pay private companies to do what you used to get for free from the state (good quality schooling, weekly rubbish collections, a local library, decent healthcare provision, etc). All of this will open up whole new avenues of investment for those billionaires desperately looking for somewhere to invest their money, as once-public services are turned into profit-making concerns.

This is the first part of the strategy. The other big problem now facing the owners of massive wealth is that their use of the third world as a source of dirt cheap labour and raw materials is seriously threatened by the shifting balance of power in the world. For five hundred years, the ruling elites running the Western world have been able to use their overwhelming firepower and technical superiority to force their own terms of trade onto the nations they impoverished in Africa, Asia and Latin America. However, this period of history is now coming to an end with the rise of places like China, India and Brazil as powerful, economically developed countries. They are not only less reliant on the export markets of the West to sell their goods, but are also increasingly demanding higher wages and fairer prices for their raw materials—and giving a lead to the rest of the global South in doing so. This threatens the ability of the world's richest to continue making money out of global poverty in the way they have been doing for generations.

All this is increasingly pushing the billionaire bankers and the governments to which they dictate policy in the direction of war. Only war can reverse the tide of economic development in the third world, and ultimately only war can destroy enough of the world's surplus capital (products, housing, factories, etc.) to pave the way for a successful new round of profitable investment.

We have been here before. Capitalism always has periodic booms and crashes, but there have only been two crashes gigantic enough to bring about the near total collapse of the world economy similar to that we face today. The first was the "Great Depression" of 1870—1896, and the second the "Great Depression" of the 1930s. Both had the same causes as today's crisis—the drying up of profitable avenues for investment—and both were ultimately 'solved' by colonialism and world war, the second of which was so successful a solution, that it paved the way for the "golden era" of capitalism—an unprecedented two-decade long boom period of growth based on rebuilding what had been destroyed in the world's biggest ever mass slaughter.

This is the context in which we have to see Britain, the U.S. and France's destruction of Libya. Anyone who thinks the British ruling class was momentarily distracted from dealing with its profitability

Sirte, Libya, after pounding by NATO 'hellfire' missiles

crisis by a small group of Arabs in distress is living in cloud cuckoo land. Fifty thousand bombing raids were carried out against Libya, totally destroying huge swathes of advanced infrastructure, not to mention entire cities (in the case of Sirte) and thousands of people. Within days of the conquest of Tripoli, Britain's Defence Minister Philip Hammond was calling on British companies to "pack their suit-cases and head for Libya" in search of the lucrative "reconstruction" contracts that will soon be dished out by NATO's puppet government. Furthermore, in destroying Libya—a wealthy oil state which was the continent's leading force pushing for African unity and economic independence, and had $30 billion set aside for African development and a new African currency—the old imperial states are intending to put the clock back on African development for generations. Further-more, Libya will likely soon host the first sizable African base for the U.S.'s new AFRICOM section of the U.S. army, set up in 2007 to invade African countries. This is part of the overall drive to use war in order to resolve this crisis of profitability, a war ultimately aimed at China, but likely to take in Syria, Iran, Algeria, South Africa and Venezuela along the way.

David Cameron is, for once, telling the truth, when he says "Whatever it takes to help our businesses take on the world—we'll do it". 'Whatever it takes' means not only the destruction of our public services; it also means the destruction of entire countries. We need to recognise that the attacks on public services and living standards here in Britain is part of a much bigger picture—the class warfare being waged by the rich against the poor, and especially against the most organised and independent sections of the third world. The constant warfare waged by the Western world for the last ten years has all been part of this struggle to maintain the class power and privilege of the dominant elites.

THEIR ONLY SOLUTION IS POVERTY AND WAR

There are many in the third world who are resisting this onslaught, and we need to make common cause with them. When the next victim is being lined up for destruction by the media propaganda machine, we need to stand in solidarity with those under attack. We should learn the lessons of the destruction of Libya, a war which was sold to us with lies even more preposterous than those used to justify the destruction of Iraq. Do you remember the stories about 10,000 killed by Gaddafi in Benghazi? According to Amnesty International, the true figure was 110—including those killed by the rebels—who we now know were armed from the first day of the insurrection. Do you remember the claims that Gaddafi was feeding his soldiers Viagra so they could carry out mass rape? Again, after looking into these allegations for months, Amnesty could not find a *single* credible case of rape by government troops. Do you remember the claims that Gaddafi had carried out aerial assaults against Tripoli? This too was false—as later verified by Russian satellite pictures. Do you remember the reports about rebel militias rounding up and lynching innocent African migrant workers by the dozen, from the very start of the revolt? Of course you don't—although true, they were rarely reported. "But surely Gaddafi was a bad man" many people say. Even if this were true—and there are millions of Libyans who would dispute this—it is surely better to live in a functioning, peaceful and prosperous country with a bad leader, than in a dysfunctional wreck of a society like those that have been created in Iraq or Afghanistan.

But there is plenty of hope in the world. Latin America has been at the forefront of a successful, popular and organised rejection of the rape of their continent by the financial institutions of the

Western world. Every major economy on the continent—with the sole exception of Colombia—is now governed by popular movements committed to the use of their natural wealth and labour to raise living standards for all, rather than simply as sources of profit for financial vampires. Venezuela's slum dwellers now have free healthcare and education—and a constitution they actually helped to draft—for the first time ever. These governments have been involved in discussions with other independent-minded third-world countries—including China, Iran and Libya before the invasion—about how to defend themselves against the war and poverty long imposed on them. We need to learn from and unite with these movements—and, above all, to reject any attempts by our own government to try to destroy them by force. ☐

The views expressed here are only those of myself, Dan Glaze-brook, and do not necessarily represent those of the movement as a whole...

The Occupy movement provides a forum for all those disgusted with the exploitation, degradation and war they see being imposed by the world's financial elites to come together and share their thoughts, analyses and strategies. Get involved and join the movement to end the dictatorship of capital.

The West aims to turn the entire global South into a failed state

Originally published by Dissident Voice, 8 December 2011

THE economic collapse that began in 2008, that was duly declared unpredictable and thoroughly unforeseen across the entire Western media, was in fact anything but. Indeed, the capitalist cycle of expansion and collapse has repeated itself so often, over hundreds of years, that its existence is openly accepted across the whole spectrum of economic thought, including in the mainstream—which refers to it, in deliberately understated terms, as the "business cycle". Only those who profit from our ignorance of this dynamic—the billionaire profiteers and their paid stooges in media and government—try to deny it.

A slump occurs when "capacity outstrips demand"—that is to say, when people can no longer afford to buy all that is being produced. This is inevitable in a capitalist system, where productive capacity is privately owned, because the global working class as a whole are never paid enough to purchase all that they collectively produce. As a result, unsold goods begin to pile up, and production facilities, such as factories, get closed down. People are thrown out of work as a result, their incomes decline, and the problem gets worse. This is exactly what we are seeing happen today.

In these circumstances, avenues for profitable investment dry up—the holders of capital can find nowhere safe to invest their money. For them, this is the crisis—not the unemployment, the famine, the poverty etc. (which, after all, remain an endemic feature of the global capitalist economy even during the "boom times", albeit on a somewhat reduced scale). The governments under their control—through ownership of the media, currency manipulation and control of the economy—must then set to work *creating* new profit-able investment opportunities.

One way they do this is by killing off public services, and thus creating opportunities for investment in the private companies that replace them. In the 1980s Britain, Margaret Thatcher privatised steel, coal, gas, electricity, water, and much else besides. In the short term, this plunged millions into unemployment, as factories and mines were closed down, and in the long term it resulted in massive price rises for basic services. But it had its intended effect—it provided valuable investment opportunities (for those with capital to spare) at a time when such opportunities were scarce, and created a long-term source of fabulous profits. This summer, for example, saw the formerly publicly owned gas company Centrica hiking its prices by another 18% to bring in a £1.3billion profit.[1] The raised prices will see many thousands more pensioners than usual die from the cold this winter as a result,[2] but gas—like all commodities in capitalist society—is not there to provide heat, but to increase capital.

In the global South, privatisation was harsher still. Bodies like the IMF and the World Bank used the leverage provided by the debt-extortion mechanism (whereby interest rates were hiked on unpayable loans that had rarely benefited the population, often taken out by corrupt rulers imposed by Western governments in the first place)[3] to force governments across Asia, Africa and Latin America to cut public spending on even basics such as health and education,[4] along with agricultural subsidies.[5] This contributed massively to the staggering rates of infant mortality and deaths from preventable disease, as well as to the AIDS epidemic now raging across Africa. But again the desired end for those imposing the policies was achieved, as new markets were created and holders of giant capital reserves could now invest in private companies to provide the services no longer available from the state.[6] The profit system was given a new lease of life, its collapse staved off once again.

The World Bank's closure of the Indian government's grain rationing and distribution service, for example, meant that a scheme providing affordable grain to all Indian citizens was closed down,[7] allowing private companies to come in and sell grain at massively increased prices (sometimes up to ten times higher). Whilst this has led to huge numbers of Indians being priced out of the market, and a resulting 200 million people now facing starvation in India, it has also led to record profits for the giant private companies now holding the world's grain stocks—which is the whole point.[8]

This round of global privatisation from the 1980s onwards, however, was so thorough that when the 2008 crisis hit, there were few state functions left to privatise. Creating investment opportunities now is much trickier than it was thirty years ago, because so much of what is *potentially* profitable is already being thoroughly exploited as it is.

In Europe, what is left of public services is hastily being dismantled, as right-wing political leaders happily privatise what is left of the public sector, and currency speculators use their firepower to pick off any country that attempts to resist. David Cameron, following the path forced on the global South over recent decades, for example, is busy opening up Britain's National Health Service to private companies,[9] and massively cutting back on public service provision for vulnerable groups such as the elderly and the jobless.[10]

> In Europe, what is left of public services is hastily being dismantled, as right-wing political leaders happily privatise what is left of the public sector, and currency speculators use their firepower to pick off any country that attempts to resist.

Across much of the global South, however, there is little left for the West to privatise, as successive IMF policies have long ago forced those countries in their grip to strip their public services to the bone (and beyond) already.

But there is one state function which, if fully privatised across the world, would make the profits made even from essentials such as healthcare and education look like peanuts. That is the most basic and essential state function of all, indeed the whole raison d'etre for the state: security.

Private security companies are one of the few growth areas during times of global recession,[11] as growing unemployment and poverty leads to increased social unrest and chaos, and those with wealth become more nervous about protecting both themselves, and their assets. Furthermore, as the Chinese economy advances at a rate of knots,[12] military superiority is fast becoming the West's only "competitive advantage"—the one area in which its expertise remains significantly ahead of its rivals. Turning this advantage, therefore, into an opportunity for investment and profit on a large scale is now one of the chief tasks facing the rulers of Western economies.

A recent article in the Guardian noted that British private security firm Group 4 is now "Europe's largest private sector employer",[13] employing 600,000 people—50% more than make up the total armed forces of Britain and France combined. With growth last year of 9% in their "new markets" division, the company have "already benefited from the unrest in north Africa and the Middle East". Group 4 are set to make a killing in Libya, following the total breakdown of security, likely to last for decades, resulting from NATO's incineration of the country's armed forces and wholesale destruction of its state apparatus. With the rule of law replaced by warfare between rival gangs of rebels, and no realistic prospect of a functioning police force for the foreseeable future, those Libyans able to manoeuvre themselves into positions of wealth and power will likely have to rely on private security for many years to come.

When Philip Hammond, Britain's new Defence Secretary and a multi-millionaire businessman himself, suggested that British companies "pack their suitcases and head to Libya", it was not only oil and construction companies he had in mind, but private security companies.

Private military companies are also becoming huge business—most notoriously, the U.S. company Blackwater,[14] renamed Xe Services after its original name became synonymous with the massacres committed by its forces in Iraq. In the U.S., Blackwater has already taken over many of the security functions of the state—charging the Department of Homeland Security $1000 per day per head in New Orleans after Hurricane Katrina, for example. "When you ship overnight, do you use the postal service or do you use FedEx?" asked Erik Prince, founder and chairman of Blackwater. "Our corporate goal is to do for the national security apparatus what FedEx did to the postal service". Another Blackwater official commented that "None of us loves the idea that devastation became a business opportunity. It's a distasteful fact. But that's what it is. Doctors, lawyers, funeral directors, even newspapers—they all make a living off of bad things happening. So do we, because somebody's got to handle it."

The danger comes when the economic climate is such that the world's most powerful governments feel they must do all they can to *create* such business opportunities. During the Cold War, the U.S. military acted (as indeed it still does) to keep the global South in a state of poverty by attacking any government that seriously sought to challenge this poverty, and imposing governments that would crush trade unions and keep the population cowed.[15] This created investment opportunities because it kept the majority of the world's labour force in conditions so desperate they were willing to work for peanuts.[16] But now this is not enough. In slump conditions, it doesn't matter how cheap your workforce is if nobody is buying your products.[17] To create the requisite business opportunities today—a large global market for its military expertise—Western governments must impose not only poverty, but also devastation. Devastation is the quickest route to converting the West's military prowess into a genuine business opportunity that can create a huge new avenue for investment when all others are drying up. And this is precisely what is happening. David Cameron is, for once, telling the truth, when he says "Whatever it takes to help our businesses take on the world—we'll do it."

Private security is one of the few industries in which the Western world still has a competitive advantage.

PHOTO: CRITICAL INTERVENTION SERVICES/PRN/NEWSCOM

As The Times put it recently, "In Iraq, the postwar business boom is not oil. It is security." In both Iraq and Afghanistan, a situation of chronic and enduring instability and civil war has been created by a very precise method.[18] Firstly, the existing state power is totally destroyed. Next, the possibility of utilising the country's domestic expertise to rebuild state capacity is undermined by barring former officials from working for the new government (a process known in Iraq as "de-Ba'athification"). Linked to this, the former ruling party is banned from playing any part in the political process, effectively ensuring that the largest and most organised political formation in each country has no option but to resort to armed struggle to gain influence, and thereby condemning the country to civil war. Next, vicious sectarianism is encouraged along whatever religious, ethnic and tribal divisions are available, often goaded by the covert actions of Western intelligence services.[19] Finally, the wholesale privatisation of resources ensures chronically destabilising levels of unemployment and inequality. The whole process is self-perpetuating, as the skilled and professional sections of the workforce—those with the means and connections—emigrate, leaving behind a dire skills shortage and even less chance of a functioning society emerging from the chaos.

This instability is not confined to the borders of the state which has been destroyed. In a masterfully cynical domino effect, for example, the aggression against Iraq has also helped to destabilise Syria. Three quarters of the 2 million Iraqi refugees fleeing the war in their own country have ended up in Syria, thus contributing to the pressure on the Syrian economy which is a major factor in the current unrest there.

The destruction of Libya will also have far reaching destabilising consequences across the region. As the recent United Nations Support Mission in Libya stated, "Libya had accumulated the largest known stockpile of Manpads [surface-to-air missiles] of any non-Manpad-producing country. Although thousands were destroyed during the seven-month NATO operations, there are increasing concerns over the looting and likely proliferation of these portable defence systems, as well as munitions and mines, highlighting the potential risk to local and regional stability." Furthermore, a large number of volatile African countries are currently experiencing a fragile peace secured by peacekeeping forces in which Libyan troops had been playing a vital role.[20] The withdrawal of these troops may well be damaging to the maintenance of the peace. Similarly, Libya, under Gaddafi's rule, had contributed generously to African development projects; a policy which will certainly be ended under the NTC—again, with potentially destabilising consequences.

Clearly, a policy of devastation and destabilisation fuels not only the market for private security, but also for arms sales—where, again, the U.S., Britain and France remain market leaders.[21] And a policy of devastation through blitzkrieg fits in clearly with the big three current long term strategic objectives of Western policy planners:

1. To corner as large a share as possible of the world's diminishing resources, most importantly oil, gas and water. A government of a devastated country is at the mercy of the occupying country when it comes to contracts. Gaddafi's Libya, for example, drove a notoriously hard bargain with the Western powers over oil contracts—acting as a key force in the 1973 oil price spike, and still in 2009 being accused by the Financial Times of "resource nationalism". But the new NTC government in Libya have been hand picked[22] for their subservience to foreign interests[23]—and know that their continued positions depend on their willingness to continue in this role.

2. To prevent the rise of the global South, primarily through the destruction of any independent regional powers (such as Iran, Libya, Syria etc.) and the destabilisation, isolation and encirclement of the rising global powers (in particular China and Russia).[24]

3. To overcome or limit the impact of economic collapse by using superior military force to create and conquer new markets through the destruction and rebuilding of infrastructure and the elimination of competition.[25]

This policy of total devastation represents a departure from the Cold War policies of the Western powers. During the Cold War, whilst the major strategic aims remained the same, the methods were different. Independent regional powers in the global South were still destabilised and invaded—and regularly—but generally with the aim of installing "compliant dictatorships". Thus, Lumumba was overthrown and replaced with Mobutu; Sukarno with Suharto; Allende with Pinochet; etc., etc. But the danger with this "imposed strongmen" policy was that strongmen can become defiant. Saddam Hussein illustrated this perfectly. After having been backed for over a decade by the West, he turned on their stooge monarchy in Kuwait. Governments that are *in* control can easily get *out of control*. However, for as long as these strongmen were needed for the services provided by their armies (protecting investments, repressing workers struggles, etc.), they were supported. The crisis now underway in the economies of the West, however, calls for more drastic measures. And the development of private security and private mercenary companies mean that the armies provided by these strongmen are starting to be deemed no longer necessary.

Congo is a case in point. For three decades, the Western powers had supported Mobutu Sese-Seko's iron rule of the Congo. But then, in the mid-90s, they allowed him to be overthrown. However, rather than allowing the Congolese resistance forces to take power and establish an effective government, they then sponsored an invasion of the country by Uganda, Rwanda and Burundi.[26] Although these countries have now largely withdrawn their militias, they continue to sponsor proxy militias which have prevented the country seeing a moment's peace for nearly fifteen years, resulting in the biggest slaughter since the end of the Second World War, with over 5 million killed. One result of this total breakdown of functioning government has been that the Western companies that loot Congo's resources have been able to do so virtually for free. Despite being the world's largest supplier of both coltan and copper, amongst many other precious minerals, the total tax revenue on these products in 2006-2007 amounted to a puny £32 million.[27] This is surely far less than what even the most useless neo-colonial puppet would have demanded.

This completely changes the meaning of the word "government". In the Congo, the government's best efforts to stabilise and develop the country have so far proved no match for the destabilisation strategies of the West and its stooges. In Afghanistan, it is well known that the government's writ has no authority outside of Kabul, if there. But then, that is the point. The role of the governments imposed on Afghanistan, Iraq and Libya, like the one they are trying to impose on Syria, is not to govern or provide for the population at all—even that most basic of functions, security. It is simply to provide a figleaf of legitimacy for the occupation of the country and to award business contracts to the colonial powers. They literally have no other function, as far as their sponsors are concerned.

It goes without saying that this policy of devastation is turning the victimised countries into a living hell. After now more than thirty years of Western destabilisation, and ten years of outright occupation, Afghanistan is at or very near the bottom of nearly every human development indicator available, with life expectancy at 44 years and an under-five mortality rate of over one in four. Mathew White, a history professor who has recently completed a detailed survey of the humanity's worst atrocities throughout history, concluded that, without doubt, "chaos is far deadlier than tyranny". It is a truth to which many Iraqis can testify. □

Britain and
the Arab Spring

Originally published in Al Ahram Weekly, 30 August 2012

OVER the past year, the British government have bombed rebels into power in Libya—and are desperately hoping to do the same in Syria—whilst simultaneously aiding and abetting the crushing of rebel forces in Bahrain and Saudi Arabia.[1] Some commentators have called this hypocritical. In fact, there is no contradiction: The British government is engaged in a vicious, region-wide attack on all independent, anti-colonial forces in the region, be they states or opposition movements. Client regimes—in many cases monarchies originally imposed by the British Empire—have been propped up, and states outside the orbit of Western control have been targeted for destruction. The policy, in other words, has been entirely consistent: a drive towards the total capitulation of the Arab world; and more specifically the destruction of any potential organised resistance to an attack on Iran. What is more, it has been planned for a long time.

The Arab Spring did not come out of the blue; it was both predictable and predicted. All demographic, economic and political trends pointed in the direction of a period of instability and civil unrest across the region, and especially in Egypt. The combination of growing and youthful populations, rising unemployment, corruption and unrepresentative government made some kind of mass manifestation of frustration a virtual certainty—as was recognised by a far-reaching speech by MI6-turned-BP operative Mark Allen in February 2009.[2] In August 2010, Barack Obama issued Presidential Study Directive Number 11, which noted "evidence of growing citizen discontent with the region's regimes" and warned that "the region is entering a critical period of transition". Four months later, Mohamed

31

Bouazizi set himself on fire in Tunisia, sparking off the unrest that led
to the downfall of President Ben-Ali.

For the world's imperial powers, wracked by their own economic crises—Britain, France and the U.S.—it was clear that this
unrest would present both a danger and an opportunity. Whilst it
threatened to disrupt the Gulf monarchies imposed by Britain during

> *Both Libya and
> Syria have long been
> considered thorns in
> the side of Western
> world domination.*

the colonial period (Bahrain, Qatar, Saudi
Arabia, Kuwait et al), it could also create
the ideal cover for the launching of long-
planned proxy wars against old enemies.

Both Libya and Syria have long been
considered thorns in the side of Western
world domination. It is not only their pol-
icies—from Gaddafi's consistent opposition to U.S. and British military bases in Africa to Assad's support for Palestinian liberation
groups—which riles Western policy makers, but the mere fact that they
have *independent* governments which are *able* to formulate and implement such policies. In the eyes of the world's unelected and unde-
clared ruling elites, for a government of the global South to be either
strong *or* independent might be just about tolerable—but not both.

Secret Anglo-American plans for the overthrow of the Syrian
government—using proxy forces directed by Western intelligence, and
carried out under the cover of 'internal disturbances'—have been in
place since at least 1957.[3] More recently, the U.S. has embarked on
a policy of funding sectarian Salafi militias to wage war against the
region's Shi'ites in order to undermine Iran, destroy the Syrian state
and cut off Hezbollah's supply lines. This policy was a direct response
to the two major setbacks in 2006—the massive wave of attacks on
Western forces by Sunni militants in Iraq and Israel's defeat in its war
with Hezbollah. In a prophetic piece in 2007, Seymour Hersh shows
how the U.S., Israel and the Saudis hatched a plan to 'redirect' Sunni
militias away from their fight against the U.S. and towards Syria. As
one U.S. government consultant put it, "it's not that we don't want
the Salafis to throw bombs; it's who they throw them at—Hezbollah,
Moqtada al-Sadr, Iran, and at the Syrians, if they continue to work
with Hezbollah and Iran".

The coming of the 'Arab Spring' provided the perfect cover for
the throwing of these bombs—and for the British and U.S. government

plans to be put into effect. They acted quickly; armed[4] attacks[5] began in both countries within days of the 'protest movement' erupting, carried out by insurgents with longstanding links to British intelligence and increasingly trained[6] and directed[7] by the SAS and MI6.[8]

Acting under the cover of the Arab Spring also proved a winning formula for Western governments to mobilise support for 'humanitarian intervention'—the twenty-first century white man's burden. Bush and Blair had given Western warmongering in the Middle East a bad name, but by implementing proxy wars—and aerial blitzkrieg—under the guise of "support for popular uprisings", it was possible to ensure that liberals and "socialists" by and large fell in line. Frustrated Western radicals, desperate to vicariously experience the "revolution" they know they would never—and let's face it, would never *want* to—actually be involved in, lapped up the imagery of the "people versus the dictator". These "useful idiots" all helpfully provided a veneer of credibility to the new wars that was clearly lacking in the case of Iraq.

The method of "proxy war"—using militias recruited from the local population to fight for imperial interests—has long been the favoured policy of British policy planners—in contrast to the more "gung-ho" boots on the ground methods of the U.S. The war against Libya gave the "Arabists" who dominate the British Foreign Office (the FCO) a chance to show the Americans how it is done. They have always preferred to cultivate local allies on the ground to do the fighting and dying—it's cheaper, less unpopular at home, and so much more subtle than the blunt, blundering and cretinous approach of the Bushblair posse. Indeed, the FCO opposed the Iraq war for precisely this reason—there was no moral, nor even strategic, disagreement— but a tactical one.[9] The perceived failure and cost (in both blood and treasure) of Iraq thus allowed the "Arabists" to gain the upper hand for the next round of colonial war that is now unfolding.

Meanwhile, client regimes—those monarchies established by Britain in the dying days of Ottoman control of the region—were given all the help they needed to drown their own uprisings in blood. Britain sold Saudi Arabia no less than £1.75 billion worth of arms last year—arms that are now being used against protesters in both Saudi Arabia and Bahrain, where the Saudis invaded last autumn to crush the growing democratic revolt, as well as to arm the militias fighting in Syria. Qatar under the absolute rule of the Al-Thani family—chosen by Britain to run the country in the mid-nineteenth century—has also been crucial in fomenting the new imperial wars. The Al- Jazeera TV channel, which plays such an important role in the colonisers' propaganda war—is run from Qatar and essentially took over the role of the BBC Arabic service when it closed operations in 1996. Qatar has also been at the forefront of the coordination, training and arming of the paramilitary proxy forces in Libya and Syria.

To ascertain the British government's attitude towards an uprising in a state in the Middle East, one simply has to ask: Is this a state created by Britain, or one built on an independent support base? Countries in the latter category get attacked, whilst those in the former are aided in consolidating their power and crushing the opposition.

Egypt, however, does not fit so neatly into either category. Egypt under Mubarak was neither a total stooge regime nor fully independent; neither a Libya nor a Qatar. Although the country had freed itself from its' British-imposed king in 1952, since the Israeli peace accord of 1979 it had been widely viewed as a client state of the U.S. and a key ally of Israel. Mubarak's standing in the Arab world reached a nadir during the Israeli onslaught against Gaza in 2008-2009, which even became known as the "Mubarak massacre" for his refusal to open the border to fleeing Palestinians. Nevertheless, imposing regime change on Libya was going to be difficult for the West with Mubarak in charge next door. He had developed a friendly relationship with Gaddafi over the years,[10] and seemed to be moving closer to Iran.[11] A UN report in 2006 even accused him of training the Islamic Courts Union[12]—the Somali government which the U.S. were working so hard to destroy—and he, along with Gaddafi, had opposed the expansion of AFRICOM—the U.S. military's "Africa Command"—on the continent.[13] A client who thinks he can conduct his own foreign policy is clearly missing the point. Removing Mubarak whilst keeping intact rule of his country by a military in hoc to the U.S. may have come to be seen as the preferred option in London and Washington –especially if this option were to divide the revolutionary movement and take the wind out of its sails. □

Part Three

The Struggle Against Third World Development

NATO's war against Libya

A war against
African development

Originally published by Counterpunch, 6 September 2011

"**A**FRICA the key to global economic growth"; this was a refreshingly honest recent headline from the Washington Post, but hardly one that qualifies as "news". African labour and resources—as any decent economic historian will tell you—has been key to global economic growth for centuries.

When the Europeans discovered America 500 years ago, their economic system went viral. Increasingly, European powers realised that the balance of power at home would be dictated by the strength they were able to draw from their colonies abroad. Imperialism (aka capitalism) has been the fundamental hallmark of the world's economic structure ever since.

For Africa, this has meant nonstop subjection to an increasingly systematic plunder of people and resources that has been unrelenting to this day. First was the brutal kidnapping of tens of millions of Africans to replace the indigenous American workforce that had been wiped out by the Europeans. The slave trade was devastating for African economies, which were rarely able to withstand the population collapse; but the capital it created for plantation owners in the Caribbean laid the foundations for Europe's industrial revolution.[1] Throughout the eighteenth and nineteenth centuries, as more and more precious materials were found in Africa (especially tin, rubber, gold and silver), the theft of land and resources ultimately resulted in the so-called "Scramble for Africa" of the 1870s, when, over the course of a few years, Europeans divided up the entire continent (with the exception of Ethiopia) amongst themselves. By this point, the world's economy was increasingly becoming an integrated whole, with Africa continuing to provide the basis for European industrial development as Africans were stripped of their land and forced down gold mines and onto rubber plantations.

After the Second World War, the European powers—weakened by years of industrial-scale slaughter of one another—contrived to adapt colonialism to fit the new conditions. As liberation movements grew in strength, the European powers confronted a new economic reality: the cost of subduing the "restless natives' was approaching the value of the wealth that could be extracted from them. Their favoured solution was what Kwame Nkrumah termed "neo-colonialism"—handing over the formal attributes of political sovereignty to a trusted bunch of hand-picked cronies who would allow the economic exploitation of their countries to continue unabated. In other words, adapting colonialism so that Africans themselves were forced to shoulder the burden and cost of policing their own populations.

All across Asia, Africa and Latin America, mass movements began to demand control of their own resources, and in many places, these movements managed to gain power

In practice, it wasn't that simple. All across Asia, Africa and Latin America, mass movements began to demand control of their own resources, and in many places, these movements managed to gain power—sometimes through guerrilla struggle, sometimes through the ballot box. This led to vicious wars by the European powers—now under the leadership of their upstart protege, the U.S.—to destroy such movements. This struggle, not the so-called "Cold War", is what defined the history of post-war international relations.

So far, neo-colonialism has largely been a successful project for the Europeans and the U.S. Africa's role as provider of cheap, often slave, labour and minerals has largely continued unabated. Poverty and disunity have been the essential ingredients that have allowed this exploitation to continue. However both are now under serious threat.

Chinese investment in Africa over the past ten years has been building up African industry and infrastructure in a way that may begin to seriously tackle the continent's poverty. In China, these policies have brought about unprecedented reductions in poverty[2] and are helping to lift the country into the position it will shortly hold as the world's leading economic power.[3] If Africa follows this model, or anything like it, the West's 500-year plunder of Africa's wealth may be nearing an end.

To prevent this "threat of African development", the Europeans and the U.S. have responded in the only way they know how—militarily. Four years ago, the U.S. set up a new "command and control centre" for the military subjugation of Africa, called AFRICOM. The problem for the U.S. was that no African country wanted to host it; indeed, until very recently, Africa was unique in being the only continent in the world without a U.S. military base. And this fact is in no small part thanks to the efforts of the Libyan government.

Before Gaddafi's revolution deposed the British-backed King Idris in 1969, Libya had hosted one of the world's biggest U.S. airbases, the Wheelus Air Base; but within a year of the revolution, it had been closed down and all foreign military personnel expelled.

More recently, Gaddafi had been actively working to scupper AFRICOM. African governments that were offered money by the U.S. to host a base were typically offered double by Gaddafi to refuse it, and in 2008 this ad-hoc opposition crystallised into a formal rejection of AFRICOM by the African Union.[4]

Perhaps even more worrying for U.S. and European domination of the continent were the huge resources that Gaddafi was channelling into African development. The Libyan government was by far the largest investor in Africa's first ever satellite, launched in 2007, which freed Africa from $500 million per year in payments to European satellite companies. Even worse for the colonial powers, Libya had allocated $30 billion for the African Union's three big financial projects, aimed at ending African dependence on Western finance.[5] The African Investment Bank—with its headquarters in Libya—was to invest in African development at no interest, which would have seriously threatened the International Monetary Fund's domination of Africa—a crucial pillar for keeping Africa in its impoverished position.[6] And Gaddafi was leading the AU's development of a new gold-backed African currency, which would have cut yet another of the strings that keep Africa at the mercy of the West, with $42 billion already allocated to this project—again, much of it by Libya.

NATO's war is aimed at ending Libya's trajectory as a socialist, anti-imperialist, pan-Africanist nation at the forefront of moves to strengthen African unity and independence. The rebels have made clear their virulent racism from the very start of their insurrection, rounding up or executing thousands of black African workers and students.[7] All the African development funds for the projects described above have been "frozen" by the NATO countries and are to be handed over to their hand-picked buddies in the National Transitional Council (NTC) to spend instead on weapons to facilitate their war.

For Africa, the war is far from over. The African continent must recognise that NATO's lashing out is a sign of desperation, of impotence, of its inability to stop the inevitable rise of Africa on the world stage. Africa must learn the lessons from Libya, continue the drive towards pan-African unity, and continue to resist AFRICOM. Plenty of Libyans will still be with them when they do so. □

Please also read these two extremely important articles on Libya's role in African development and independence:
Gold, Oil, Africa and Why the West wants Gaddafi Dead by Brian E Muhammed for the Final Call[8]
Why the West wants Gaddafi Out by Jean-Paul Pougala for the Southern Times[9]

Mali, Algeria and the African Union

The West's war on African development continues

Originally published by Counterpunch, 15 February 2012

AFRICA'S classic depiction in the mainstream media, as a giant basketcase full of endless war, famine and helpless children creates an illusion of a continent utterly dependent on Western handouts. In fact, the precise opposite is true—it is the West that is reliant on African handouts. These handouts come in many and varied forms. They include illicit flows of resources,[1] the profits of which invariably find their way into the West's banking sector via strings of tax havens (as thoroughly documented in Nicholas Shaxson's Poisoned Wells). Another is the mechanism of debt-extortion whereby banks lend money to military rulers (often helped to power by Western governments, such as the Congo's former President Mobutu), who then keep the money for themselves (often in a private account with the lending bank), leaving the country paying exorbitant interest on an exponentially growing debt. Recent research by Leonce Ndikumana and James K. Boyce found that up to 80 cents in every borrowed dollar fled the borrower nation in "capital flight" within a year, never having been invested in the country at all; whilst meanwhile $20 billion per year is drained from Africa in "debt servicing" on these, essentially fraudulent, "loans".

Another handout comes via the looting of minerals. Countries like the Democratic Republic of Congo are ravaged by armed militias who steal the country's resources and sell them at sub-market prices to Western companies, with many of these militias run by neighbouring countries such as Uganda, Rwanda and Burundi who are in turn sponsored by the West, as regularly highlighted in UN reports.[2] Finally, and perhaps most importantly, are the pitifully low prices paid both for African raw materials and for the labour that mines, grows or picks them, which effectively amount to an African subsidy for Western living standards and corporate profits.[3]

This is the role for which Africa has been ascribed by the masters of the Western capitalist economy: a supplier of cheap resources and cheap labour. And keeping this labour, and these resources, cheap depends primarily on one thing: ensuring that Africa remains underdeveloped and impoverished. If it were to become more prosperous, wages would rise; if it were to become more technologically developed, it would be able to add value to its raw materials through the manufacturing process before exporting them, forcing up the prices paid. Meanwhile, extracting *stolen* oil and minerals depends on keeping African states weak and divided. The Democratic Republic of Congo, for example—whose mines produce tens of billions of mineral resources each year—were only, in one recent financial year, able to collect a paltry $32 million in tax revenues from mining due to the proxy war waged against that country by Western-backed militias.[4]

The establishment of the African Union in 2002 was potentially a threat to this setup; a more integrated, more unified African continent would be harder to exploit.

The establishment of the African Union in 2002 was potentially a threat to this setup; a more integrated, more unified African continent would be harder to exploit. Of special concern to Western strategic planners are the financial and military aspects of African unification. On a financial level, plans for an African Central Bank (to issue a single African currency, the gold-backed dinar) would greatly limit the capacity of the U.S., Britain and France to exploit the continent, threatening their ability to manipulate local currencies to their advantage and providing Africa with unprecedented financial autonomy. The other two proposed AU financial institutions—the African Investment Bank and the African Monetary Fund—could fatally undermine the ability of institutions such as the International Monetary Fund to manipulate the economic policies of African countries through their monopoly of finance. As Jean Paul Pougala has pointed out, the African Monetary Fund, with its planned startup capital of $42 billion, "is expected to totally supplant the African activities of the International Monetary Fund which, with only US$25 billion, was able to bring an entire continent to its knees and make it swallow questionable privatisation like forcing African countries to move from public to private monopolies".[5]

Along with these potentially threatening financial developments came moves on the military front. The 2004 AU Summit in Sirte, Libya, agreed on a Common African Defence and Security Charter, including an article stipulating that "any attack against an African country is considered as an attack against the Continent as a whole", mirroring the Charter of NATO itself. This was followed up in 2010 by the creation of an African Standby Force, with a mandate to uphold and implement the Charter. Clearly, if NATO was going to make any attempt to reverse African unity by force, time was running out.

Yet the creation of the African Standby Force represented not only a threat, but also an opportunity. Whilst there was certainly the possibility of the ASF becoming a genuine force for independence, resisting neocolonialism and defending Africa against imperialist aggression, there was also the possibility that, handled in the right way, and under a different leadership, the force could become the opposite—a proxy force for continued neocolonial subjugation under a Western chain of command. The stakes were—and are—clearly very high.

AFRICOM AND THE AFRICAN UNION

Meanwhile, the West had already been building up its own military preparations for Africa. Its economic decline, coupled with the rise of China, meant that it was increasingly unable to continue to rely on economic blackmail and financial manipulation alone in order to keep the continent subordinated and weak.[6] Comprehending clearly that this meant it would be increasingly forced into military action to maintain its domination, a U.S. white paper published in 2002 by the African Oil Policy Initiative Group recommended "A new and vigorous focus on U.S. military cooperation in sub-Saharan Africa, to include design of a sub-unified command structure which could produce significant dividends in the protection of U.S. investments". This structure came into existence in 2008, under the name of AFRICOM. The costs—economic, military and political—of direct intervention in Iraq and Afghanistan, however—with the costs of the Iraq war alone estimated at over three trillion dollars[7]—meant that AFRICOM was supposed to primarily rely on local troops to do the fighting and dying.[8] AFRICOM was to be the body which coordinated the subordination of African armies under a Western chain of command; which turned, in other words, African armies into Western proxies.

The biggest obstacle to this plan was the African Union itself, which categorically rejected any U.S. military presence on African soil in 2008—forcing AFRICOM to house its headquarters in Stuttgart, Germany, a humiliating about turn after President Bush had already publicly announced his intention to set up the HQ in Africa. Worse was to come in 2009, when Colonel Gaddafi—the continent's staunchest advocate of anti-imperialist policies—was elected Chairman of the AU. Under his leadership, Libya had already become the biggest financial donor to the African Union, and he was now proposing a fast-track process of African integration, including a single African army, currency and passport.

His fate is clearly now a matter of public record. After mounting an invasion of his country based on a pack of lies worse than those told about Iraq, NATO reduced Libya to a devastated failed state and facilitated its leader's torture and execution, thus taking out their number one opponent.[9] For a time, it appeared as though the African

U.S. Seabees training in preparation for deployment, including to the Horn of Africa, 2009.

PHOTO: NICHOLAS LINGO

Union had been tamed. Three of its members—Nigeria, Gabon and South Africa—had voted in favour of military intervention at the UN Security Council, and its new chairman—Jean Ping—was quick to recognize the new Libyan government imposed by NATO, and to downplay and denigrate his predecessor's achievements.[10] Indeed, he even forbade the African Union assembly from observing a minute's silence for Gaddafi after his murder.

However, this did not last. The South Africans, in particular, quickly came to regret their support for the intervention, with both President Zuma and Thabo Mbeki making searing criticisms of NATO in the months that followed.[11] Zuma argued—correctly—that NATO had acted illegally by blocking the ceasefire and negotiations that had been called for by the UN resolution, had been brokered by the AU, and had been agreed to by Gaddafi. Mbeki went much further and argued that the UN Security Council, by ignoring the AU's proposals, were treating "the peoples of Africa with absolute contempt" and that "the Western powers have enhanced their appetite to intervene on our continent, including through armed force, to ensure the protection of their interests, regardless of our views as Africans". A senior diplomat in the South African Foreign Ministry's Department of International Relations said that "most SADC (Southern African Development Community) states, particularly South Africa, Zimbabwe, Angola, Tanzania, Namibia and Zambia which played a key role in the Southern African liberation struggle, were not happy with the way Jean Ping handled the Libyan bombing by NATO jets". In July 2012, Ping was forced out and replaced—with the support of 37 African states—by Dr. Nkosazana Dlamini-Zuma: former South African Foreign Minister, Thabo Mbeki's "right hand woman"—and clearly not a member of Ping's capitulationist camp. The African Union was once again under the control of forces committed to genuine independence.

LIBYA'S CONTRIBUTIONS TO AFRICAN SECURITY

However, Gaddafi's execution had not only taken out a powerful member of the African Union, but also the lynchpin of regional security in the Sahel—Sahara region. Using a careful mixture of force, ideological challenge and negotiation, Gaddafi's Libya was at the head of a transnational security system that had prevented Salafist militias gaining a foothold, as recognized by U.S. Ambassador Christo-

Muammar Gaddafi attends the 12th African Union Summit, Feb. 2, 2009.

pher Stevens in 2008: "The Government of Libya has aggressively pursued operations to disrupt foreign fighter flows, including more stringent monitoring of air/land ports of entry, and blunt the ideological appeal of radical Islam... Libya cooperates with neighbouring states in the Sahara and Sahel region to stem foreign fighter flows and travel of transnational terrorists. Muammar Gaddafi recently brokered a widely-publicised agreement with Tuareg tribal leaders from Libya, Chad, Niger, Mali and Algeria in which they would abandon separatist aspirations and smuggling (of weapons and transnational extremists) in exchange for development assistance and financial support... our assessment is that the flow of foreign fighters from Libya to Iraq and the reverse flow of veterans to Libya has diminished due to the Government of Libya's cooperation with other states..."

This "cooperation with other states" refers to the CEN-SAD (Community of Sahel-Saharan States), an organization launched by Gaddafi in 1998 aiming at free trade, free movement of peoples and regional development between its 23 member states, but with a primary focus on peace and security. As well as countering the influence of Salafist militias, the CEN-SAD had played a key role in mediating conflicts between Ethiopia and Eritrea, and within the Mano River region, as well as negotiating a lasting solution to the rebellion in Chad. CEN-SAD was based in Tripoli and Libya was unquestionably the dominant force in the group; indeed CEN-SAD support was primarily behind Gaddafi's election as Chairman of the AU in 2009.

The very effectiveness of this security system, was a double blow for Western hegemony in Africa: not only did it bring Africa closer to peace and prosperity, but simultaneously undercut a key pretext for Western intervention. The U.S. had established its own "Trans-Sahara Counter-Terrorism Partnership" (TSCTP), but as Muatassim Gaddafi (Libyan National Security Advisor) explained to Hillary Clinton in Washington in 2009, the "Tripoli-based Community of Sahel-Saharan States (CEN-SAD) and the North Africa Standby Force obviated TSCTP's mission".

As long as Gaddafi was in power and heading up a powerful and effective regional security system, Salafist militias in North Africa could not be used as a "threatening menace" justifying Western invasion and occupation to save the helpless natives. By actually achieving what the West claim to want (but everywhere fail to achieve)—the neutralization of "Islamist terrorism"—Libya had stripped the imperialists of a key pretext for their war against Africa. At the same time, they had prevented the militias from fulfilling their other historical function for the West—as a proxy force to destabilize independent secular states (fully documented in Mark Curtis' excellent *Secret Affairs*). The West had supported Salafi death squads in campaigns to destabilize the USSR and Yugoslavia highly successfully, and would do so again against Libya and Syria.

NORTH AFRICA FOLLOWING NATO'S VICTORY

With NATO's redrawing of Libya as a failed state, this security system has fallen apart. Not only have the Salafi militias been provided with the latest hi-tech military equipment by NATO, they have been given free reign to loot the Libyan government's armouries,[12] and provided with a safe haven from which to organize attacks across the region. Border security has collapsed, with the apparent connivance of the new Libyan government and its NATO sponsors, as this damning report from global intelligence firm Jamestown Foundation notes: "Al-Wigh was an important strategic base for the Qaddafi regime, being located close to the borders with Niger, Chad and Algeria. Since the rebellion, the base has come under the control of Tubu tribal fighters under the nominal command of the Libyan Army and the direct command of Tubu commander Sharafeddine Barka Azaiy, who complains: "During the revolution, controlling this base was of key strategic importance. We liberated it. Now we feel neglected. We do not have sufficient equipment, cars and weapons to protect the border. Even though we are part of national army, we receive no salary". The report concludes that "The Libyan GNC (Governing National Council) and its predecessor, the Transitional National Council (TNC), have failed to secure important military facilities in the south and have allowed border security in large parts of the south to effectively become "privatized" in the hands of tribal groups who are also well-known for their traditional smuggling pursuits. In turn, this has jeopardized the security of Libya's oil infrastructure and the security of its neighbours. As the sale and transport of Libyan arms becomes a mini-industry in the post-Qaddafi era...the vast amounts of cash available to al-Qaeda in the Islamic Maghreb are capable of opening many doors in an impoverished and underdeveloped region. If the French-led offensive in northern Mali succeeds in displacing the Islamist militants, there seems to be little at the moment to prevent such groups from establishing new bases in the poorly-controlled desert wilderness of southern Libya. So long as there is an absence of central control of security structures in Libya, that nation's interior will continue to present a security threat to the rest of the nations in the region."[13]

> 'During the revolution, controlling this base was of key strategic importance. We liberated it. Now we feel neglected. We do not have sufficient equipment, cars and weapons to protect the border. Even though we are part of national army, we receive no salary.'

The most obvious victim of this destabilization has been Mali. That the Salafist takeover of Mali is a direct consequence of NATO's actions in Libya is not in doubt by any serious analysts.[14] One result of the spread of NATO-backed destabilization to Mali is that Algeria— which lost 200,000 citizens in a deadly civil war between Islamist rebels and the government in the 1990s—is now surrounded by heavily armed Salafist militias on both its eastern (Libya) and southern (Mali) borders.

Following the destruction of Libya and the toppling of Mubarak, Algeria is now the only state in North Africa still governed by an anti-colonial party that won independence from European tyranny. This independent spirit is still very much in evidence in Algeria's attitude towards Africa and Europe.

On the African front, Algeria is a strong supporter of the African Union, contributing 15% of its budget, and has $16 billion committed to the establishment of the African Monetary Fund, making it the Fund's largest contributor by far. In its relations with Europe, however, it has consistently refused to play the subordinate role expected of it. Algeria and Syria were the only countries in the Arab League to vote against NATO bombings of Libya and Syria, and Algeria famously gave refuge to members of Gaddafi's family fleeing NATO's onslaught. But for European strategic planners, perhaps more worrying than all of this is that Algeria—along with Iran and Venezuela—is what they call an OPEC "hawk", committed to driving a hard bargain for their natural resources. As an exasperated article in the Financial Times recently explained, "resource nationalism" has taken hold, with the result that "Big Oil has soured on Algeria [and] companies complain of crushing bureaucracy, tough fiscal terms and the bullying behavior of Sonatrach, the state-run energy group, which has a stake in most oil and gas ventures". It goes on to note that Algeria implemented a "controversial windfall tax" in 2006, and quotes a western oil executive in Algiers as saying that "[oil] companies...have had it with Algeria". It is instructive to note that the same newspaper had also accused Libya of "resource nationalism"—that most heinous of crimes for readers of the Financial Times, it seems—barely a year before NATO's invasion.[15]   Of course, "resource nationalism" means exactly that—a nation's resources being used primarily for the benefit and development of the nation itself (rather than foreign companies)—and in that sense Algeria is indeed guilty as charged. Algeria's oil exports stand at over $70 billion per year, and much of this income has been used to invest in massive spending on health and housing, along with a recent $23 billion loan and public grants programme to encourage small business.[16] Indeed, high levels of social spending are considered by many to be a key reason why no "Arab Spring" style uprising has taken off in Algeria in recent years.

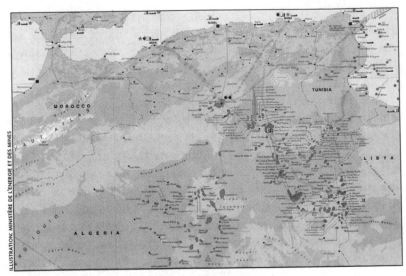

Map showing Algeria's extensive oil and gas pipeline
infrastructure, including connections to Europe.

This tendency to "resource nationalism" was also noted in
a recent piece by STRATFOR, the global intelligence firm, who wrote
that "foreign participation in Algeria has suffered in large part due to
protectionist policies enforced by the highly nationalistic military government".[17] This was particularly worrying, they argued, as Europe
is about to become a whole lot more dependent on Algerian gas as
North Sea reserves run out: "Developing Algeria as a major natural
gas exporter is an economic and strategic imperative for EU countries
as North Sea production of the commodity enters terminal decline in
the next decade. Algeria is already an important energy supplier to
the Continent, but Europe will need expanded access to natural gas
to offset the decline of its indigenous reserves." British and Dutch
North Sea gas reserves are estimated to run out by the end of the
decade, and Norway's to go into sharp decline from 2015 onwards.
With Europe fearful of overdependence on gas from Russia and Asia,
Algeria—with reserves of natural gas estimated at 4.5 trillion cubic
metres, alongside shale gas reserves of 17 trillion cubic meters—
will become essential, the piece argues. But the biggest obstacle to
European control of these resources remains the Algerian government—with its "protectionist policies" and "resource nationalism".

Without saying it outright, the piece concludes by suggesting that a destabilized "failed state" Algeria would be far preferable to Algeria under a stable independent "protectionist" government, noting that "the existing involvement of EU energy majors in high-risk countries like Nigeria, Libya, Yemen and Iraq indicates a healthy tolerance for instability and security problems." In other words, in an age of private security, Big Oil no longer requires stability or state protection for its investments: disaster zones can be tolerated; strong, independent states cannot.

It is, therefore, perceived to be in the strategic interests of Western energy security to see Algeria turned into a failed state, just as Iraq, Afghanistan and Libya have been. With this in mind, it is clear to see how the apparently contradictory policy of arming the Salafist militias one minute (in Libya) and bombing them the next (in Mali) does in fact make sense. The French bombing mission aims, in its own words, at the "total reconquest" of Mali, which in practice means driving the rebels gradually Northwards through the country— in other words, straight into Algeria.[18]

Thus the wilful destruction of the Libyan-centred Sahel-Sahara security system has had many benefits for those who wish to see Africa remain consigned to its role of underdeveloped provider of cheap raw materials. It has armed, trained, and provided territory to militias bent on the destruction of Algeria, the only major resource-rich North African state committed to genuine African unity and independence. In doing so, it has also persuaded some Africans that—in contrast to their united rejection of AFRICOM not long ago—they do, after all, now need to call on the West for "protection" from these militias. Like a classic mafia protection racket, the West makes its protection "necessary" by unleashing the very forces from which people require protection. Now France is occupying Mali, the U.S. is establishing a new drone base in Niger and David Cameron is talking about his commitment to a new "war on terror" spanning six countries, and likely to last decades.

It is not, however, all good on the imperialist front. Far from it; indeed the West had almost certainly hoped to avoid sending in their own soldiers at all. The initial aim was that Algeria would be sucked in, lured into exactly the same trap that was successfully used against the Soviet Union in the 1980s, an earlier example of

Britain and the U.S. sponsoring a violent sectarian insurgency on their enemy's borders, attempting to drag their target into a destructive war in response.[19] The USSR's war in Afghanistan ultimately not only failed but destroyed the country's economy and morale in the process, and was a key factor behind the gratuitous self-destruction of the Soviet state in 1991. Algeria, however, refused to fall into this trap, and Clinton and Hollande's good cop-bad cop routine—the former's "pressure for action" in Algiers last October[20] followed by French attempts at sucking up two months later—came to nothing.[21] Meanwhile, rather than sticking to the script, the West's unpredictable Salafi proxies expanded from their base in Northern Mali not north to Algeria as intended, but South to Bamako, threatening to unseat a Western-allied regime that had only just been installed in a coup less than a year earlier. The French were forced to intervene to drive them north and back towards the state that had been their real target all along. For now, this invasion appears to have a certain level of support amongst those Africans who fear the West's Salafi proxies more than the West's own soldiers. Once the occupation starts to drag on, boosting the credibility and numbers of the guerillas, whilst exposing the brutality of the occupiers and their allies, we will see whether that lasts. ☐

Morsi in Tehran

Strategic alignment or a safe pair of hands?

Originally published by New Statesman, 31st August 2012

EGYPT'S new President Mohammed Morsi was in China last week, putting in an appearance at the Non-Aligned Movement summit in Iran on the way home—all before ever having stepped foot in the U.S. Several commentators have speculated that his movements herald a strategic realignment for Egypt away from Washington and towards Tehran. The Washington Post hailed the trip as "a major foreign policy shift for the Arab world's most populous nation, after decades of subservience to Washington". This seems very unlikely, if not disingenuous, for a number of reasons.

Firstly, the importance of foreign visits and their chronology can easily be overstated. Every reactionary from Doha to Downing St. goes to China to do business, and China does not demand political allegiance in return; this trip in itself, therefore, signifies nothing about Egypt's foreign policy. Likewise with Tehran; the Turkish foreign minister and the Emir of Qatar are also attending the summit, yet no one seems to be suggesting that this signifies any "major foreign policy shift" on the part of either of those countries. Neither should it be forgotten that, although Morsi has yet to visit the U.S., he hosted a visit from Hillary Clinton within a fortnight of coming to power, and his first foreign visit as President was to King Abdullah of Saudi Arabia—the West's number one Arab friend.

Secondly, Morsi's government looks set to be deepening, not reducing, his country's economic dependence on the West through a $4.5 billion IMF loan currently under negotiation. As has often been discussed in these pages, the IMF do not do free lunches; they demand their pound of flesh in the form of privatisation of industry, the abolition of tariffs and subsidies and other measures to make life easier for foreign capital (and harder for the poor). Not that Morsi's organisation, the Muslim Brotherhood, have any particular objection to such policies—their economic strategy document *al-Nahda* ("the renaissance") is a model of the type of extreme neo-liberalism the IMF so adores. They have already pledged to abolish the £10 billion annual food and fuel subsidy that is currently a lifeline for the country's poor, and are committed to the emasculation of the trade unions which were such a potent force in last year's uprisings. Opposition to such measures will certainly be blunted if the Brotherhood implement their commitment to end the current reservation of 50% of seats in the Egyptian parliament for workers and farmers. This reform would pave the way to a parliament stacked with corporate-sponsored middle-class career politicians based on the Western model—complete, presumably, with similar levels of subservience to the global neoliberal agenda. Interestingly, the IMF loan currently being negotiated was rejected by Egypt's military leaders last summer as being politically unwise—in other words, likely to provoke massive popular outrage. In economic terms, the elites of Egypt and the West are definitely singing from the same songsheet.

Finally, Morsi is clearly playing the role of figurehead for the latest incarnation of the West's regime change strategy for Syria. Long before his outburst against Assad in Tehran this week, Morsi had nailed his colours to the mast, claiming that the Syrian government must "disappear from the scene" because "there is no room for talk about reform". Now he is proposing a new Contact Group for Syria involving Saudi Arabia, Turkey and Iran. That this plan was not immediately dismissed by Washington and London—as similar suggestions had been in the past—is indication enough that it has their backing.[1] Morsi's spokesman Yasser Ali explained that "Part of the mission is in China, part of the mission is in Russia and part of the mission is in Iran". Presumably there will be an attempt to win Russian and Chinese acquiescence to some kind of NATO-imposed "no-fly zone", as suggested this week by U.S. general Martin Dempsey, before delivering an ultimatum to Tehran not to intervene.

Rather than a "strategic shift", what is more likely to be happening is that Morsi is consciously allowing the idea of a "turn from Washington" to take root—with the backing of sections of the

Western media—in order to gain credibility, allowing his Syria plan to be presented as an "independent regional initiative", and thus undermine Russian and Chinese claims of Western imperialism.

We have been here before. Turkish President Erdogan gained huge prestige across the Arab world three years ago for the supposed 'anti-Zionism' he demonstrated walking out of Shimon Peres' speech at the World Economic Forum, and his grandstanding over the Israeli attack on the Gaza flotilla the following year. He went on to use this prestige, however, to garner support for the West's ongoing proxy war against Syria, the one Arab state that backs up its supportive words with material support for the Palestinian resistance. In so doing, he effectively placed himself at the vanguard of the Israeli-Western policy agenda for the region.

Morsi's Egypt remains financially dependent on the U.S., and now also Saudi Arabia. The U.S. famously provides $1.3 billion military aid annually, whilst Saudi Arabia has been the only country to provide loans to Egypt—to the tune of $4 billion—since last year's uprising. Meanwhile, the country has been suffering under the double hammer blows of world recession and the loss of tourism. Egypt's financial stability depends, in the short term at least, on keeping its two backers happy. In this light, Morsi's comments this week that his commitment to Western-sponsored regime change in Syria was a "strategic necessity" is quite a candid admission. Morsi's calculated posturing is an attempt to win credibility by appearing to distance himself from the U.S., whilst in reality he is working to win support for U.S. goals both in Egypt—through the pursuance of an extreme neoliberal economic agenda—and in the wider region, by spearheading the latest incarnation of the West's roadmap to Syrian regime change. ☐

Part Four
The Planning and Execution of the War Against Libya

NATO has been cultivating its Libyan allies since 2007

Originally published by Dissident Voice, 12 September 2012

A VIOLENT rebellion broke out in Benghazi, Libya on February 15, 2011.[1] Six days later, Libyan Justice Minister Mustafa Abdul-Jalil resigned to set up an alternative government. On February 27, the Transitional National Council was established, and on March 5, this body had declared itself the "sole representative of all Libya", with Abdul-Jalil at its head. France recognised the TNC as the legitimate Libyan government on March 10 and Britain offered them a diplomatic office on UK soil the same day. Nine days later, the Council set up a new Libyan Central Bank and National Oil Company.[2] In barely a month from the start of the rebellion, Abdul-Jalil had positioned himself as head not only of the rebels, but of the new government in waiting, with control of Libyan resources and monetary policy and the blessing of the West. On March 17, NATO began its mass slaughter of Libyan soldiers in order to install his regime.

Clearly, seasoned imperial powers such as Britain, France and the U.S., would not commit to the huge expenditure of a months-long air campaign to bring somebody to power in such a strategically important, oil rich state, unless they were already a tried and trusted asset. So who exactly is Abdul Jalil?

Abdul-Jalil gained his job in the Libyan government in January 2007, when he was named Secretary of the General People's Committee for Justice (the equivalent of Justice Minister). He has been paving the way for NATO's military and economic conquest of Libya ever since.

First, as head of the judiciary, he oversaw the release from prison of the hundreds of anti-Gaddafi fighters who went on to form the core of the insurgency. Saif al-Islam Gaddafi (Muamar's

Mark Allen—BP's MI6 man in Libya. Did he arrange Jibril and Abdul-Jalil's positions in Gaddafi's government?

son) was leading the prisoner release programme—a move he now publicly regrets as being naïve in the extreme—but faced stiff opposition from powerful elements within his own government. Having a sympathetic Justice Minister was therefore crucial to allowing the releases to go ahead smoothly. Hundreds of members of the Libyan Islamic Fighting Group—including its founder Abdulhakim Belhadj, now military chief of Tripoli—were released in 2009 and 2010, and went on to form the only trained and experienced indigenous fighting units of the rebellion.[3] In January 2010, Abdul-Jalil threatened to resign unless the prisoner release programme was sped up.[4] On the second day of the insurgency, the final batch of 110 members of the LIFG were released; his work done, Abdul-Jalil quit his role of Justice Minister soon after to set up the TNC.

Second, Abdul-Jalil was able to use his position to help prepare the legal framework for the corporate takeover of Libyan resources that was enacted so swiftly after the creation of the TNC. Although his official role was head of the judiciary, a large part of the dialogue between Abdul-Jalil and U.S. officials recorded in leaked U.S. diplomatic cables focused on privatisation of the economy. These reported Abdul-Jalil's enthusiasm for "private sector involvement", and revealed his belief that this would require regime change, or as the cables euphemistically put it, "international assistance", to fully achieve. The cables also reported Abdul-Jalil's ominous comment that, on the matter of creating a "sound commercial legal environment" and improving relations between Libya and the U.S., "less talk and more action was needed".[5]

Thirdly, Abdul-Jalil was able to arrange "below-the-radar" covert meetings between the pro-privatisation Libyans in the "Commercial Law Development Programme" and U.S. officials, both in the U.S. and in Libya. The leaked U.S. cables praised his "willingness to allow his staff to communicate with emboffs (Embassy officials) outside of official channels" and noted that "his organization seems to have a parallel track in securing visa approvals, bypassing Protocol and the MFA (Ministry for Foreign Affairs)".[6]

Shortly after Abdul-Jalil's appointment in 2007, the other key player in today's TNC—President Mahmoud Jibril—was also given a government job in Libya. Jibril was made Head of the National Planning Council and later Head of the National Economic Development Board where, according to the U.S. cables, he too helped to "pave the way" for the privatisation of Libya's economy and "welcomed American companies". U.S. officials were positively ecstatic about Jibril after their meeting in May 2009, concluding that "With a PhD in strategic planning from the University of Pittsburgh, Jibril is a serious interlocutor who 'gets' the U.S. perspective". Very revealing given the spate of ambassador defections that followed the Benghazi rebellion was the additional revelation that Jibril had been helping to facilitate six U.S. training programmes for diplomats.[7]

It also turned out that 2007 was a crucial year for the other big player in today's TNC, Head of Tripoli's Military Council, Abdulhakim Belhadj. Belhadj was the founder of the Libyan Islamic Fighting Group, an Al-Qaeda affiliate which launched an armed insurrection against the Libyan state in 1995 lasting for two years. His release from prison in Libya in March 2010, along with hundreds of other LIFG fighters, was the culmination of a process that began with an open letter published in November 2007 by Norman Benotman—one of the group's many fighters who had been given a safe haven in the UK since the failed uprising. His letter renounced violence and, according to the London Times, "asked Al-Qaeda to give up all its operations in the Islamic world and in the West, adding that ordinary westerners were blameless and should not be attacked". The letter led to a process of dialogue between the LIFG and the Libyan government, and was followed up two years later by an apology by the LIFG for their anti-government violence in the past, and a statement that "the reduction of jihad to fighting with the sword is an error and shortcoming".[8] They had clearly come to realise that drones and B52 bombers would be far more effective.

So 2007 was the year that launched these three men on the path towards their current role as NATO's proxy rulers in Libya. Benotman's letter made NATO support for a violent Al-Qaeda affiliate politically possible, and helped to sucker Saif al-Islam into releasing the very people who would become the ground forces in the overthrow of his government. Abdul-Jalil's appointment as Justice Minister smoothed over the fighters' release, and prepared the legal framework for an economic takeover by Western corporations. Jibril's appointment as Planning Minister prepared, at a micro-level, the detail of how this takeover would come about, and cultivated the relationships with the Western companies that would be invited in.

> *Jibril's appointment as Planning Minister prepared, at a micro-level, the detail of how this takeover would come about, and cultivated the relationships with the Western companies that would be invited in.*

So why did all this come about? Who was pulling the strings?

In the case of Benotman's letter, this would have been a fairly simple matter of MI6 contacting him in London, where he lived, and putting him in touch with a decent PR firm to help draft the letter that would make it politically possible for NATO to set itself up as the LIFG's airforce.

As for the two government appointments, Saif al-Islam Gaddafi was ultimately responsible, but he was clearly not intending the outcome that resulted. He was implementing political and economic reforms driven by both genuine belief, and a naïve desire to improve relations between his government and the West; he did not realise that he was unwittingly laying the ground for the political and economic destruction of his country. So the question is—was he acting on somebody else's advice?

If he was, the most likely candidate is Mark Allen.

Mark Allen was the MI6 agent who had facilitated Libya's 'rapprochement' with the West in 2003. Saif al-Islam had led the negotiations on the Libyan side, so by 2007, the two men knew each other quite well. But by then, Allen was no longer officially employed by MI6. In 2004, he had been fast tracked by the British Cabinet Office, bypassing the usual security procedures, to work for BP and in 2007, he successfully concluded a massive £15 billion oil deal between BP and the Libyan government.[9] Could the appointment of Abdul-Jalil and Mahmoud Jibril have been part of this deal? In hindsight, given their subsequent roles, it seems highly likely that MI6 would have used whatever leverage it could to manoeuvre willing accomplices into positions inside the Libyan government.

According to the Daily Mail, Allen was also actively involved in pressuring the UK government to support the prisoner release programme.[10] Of course, the tone of their article, as with the current media furore about MI6 complicitity in Belhadj's torture, all fit in with the overall narrative that Gaddafi and the West had a great relationship until the rebellion started and forced NATO to conduct a humanitarian intervention. This bizarre thesis is designed to obscure the reality that Libya under Gaddafi's leadership was an obstacle to Western domination and subordination of Africa, and that MI6 has been plotting his removal ever since he came to power. □

Libya, Africa and AFRICOM

An ongoing
disaster

Originally published by Z Magazine, 25 May 2012

THE scale of the ongoing tragedy visited on Libya by NATO and its allies is becoming clearer with each passing day. The destruction of the state's forces by British, French and American blitzkrieg has left the country in a state of total chaos—and with nothing to unite them other than a temporary willingness to act as NATO's foot soldiers, the former "rebels" are now turning on each other. In southern Libya, 147 were killed as a result of in-fighting in a single week earlier this year,[1] and in recent weeks government buildings—including the Prime Ministerial compound—have come under fire by "rebels" demanding cash payment for their services.[2] $1.4 billion has been paid out already—demonstrating once again that it was the forces of NATO colonialism, not Gaddafi, who were reliant on "mercenaries"—but payments were suspended last month due to widespread nepotism.[3] Indeed, corruption is fast becoming endemic—a further $2.5 billion in oil revenues that was supposed to have been transferred to the national treasury remains unaccounted for.[4] Libyan resources are now being jointly plundered by the oil multinationals and a handful of chosen families from amongst the country's new elites; a classic neo-colonial stitch-up.[5] The use of these resources for giant infrastructure projects such as the Great Manmade River, and the massive raising of living standards over the past four decades (Libyan life expectancy rose from 51 to 77 since Gaddafi came to power in 1969) sadly looks to have already become a thing of the past.[6]

But woe betide anyone who mentions that now. It was decided long ago that no supporters of Gaddafi would be allowed to stand in the upcoming elections, but recent changes have gone even further.

Law 37, passed by the new NATO-imposed government last month, has created a new crime of "glorifying" the former government or its leader—subject to a maximum sentence of life imprisonment. Would this include a passing comment that things were better under Gaddafi? The law is cleverly vague enough to be open to interpretation. It is a recipe for institutionalised political persecution.

Even more indicative of the contempt for the rule of law amongst the new government—a government, remember, which has yet to receive any semblance of popular mandate, and whose only power base remains the colonial armed forces—is Law 38. This law has now guaranteed immunity from prosecution for anyone who committed crimes aimed at "promoting or protecting the revolution". Those responsible for the ethnic cleansing of Tawergha—such as Misrata's self-proclaimed "brigade for the purging of black skins"—can continue their hunting down of that cities' refugees in the full knowledge that they have the new "law" on their side. Those responsible for the massacres in Sirte and elsewhere have nothing to fear. Those involved in the widespread torture of detainees can continue without repercussions—so long as it is aimed at "protecting the revolution"—i.e. maintaining NATO-TNC dictatorship.

This is the reality of the new Libya: Civil war, squandered resources, and societal collapse, where voicing preference for the days when Libya was prosperous and at peace is a crime, but lynching and torture is not only permitted but encouraged.

Nor has the disaster remained a national one. Libya's destabilisation has already spread to Mali, prompting a coup, and huge numbers of refugees—especially amongst Libya's large black migrant population—have fled to neighbouring countries in a desperate attempt to escape both aerial destruction and lynch mob rampage, putting further pressure on resources elsewhere. Many Libyan fighters, their work done in Libya, have now been shipped by their imperial masters to Syria to spread their sectarian violence there too.

Most worrying for the African continent, however, is the forward march of AFRICOM—the U.S. military's African command—in the wake of the aggression against Libya. It is no coincidence that barely a month after the fall of Tripoli—and in the same month Gaddafi was murdered (October 2011)—the U.S. announced it was sending troops to no less than four more African countries—the Central African

Republic, Uganda, South Sudan and the Democratic Republic of Congo. AFRICOM have now announced an unprecedented fourteen major joint military exercises in African countries for 2012. The military re-conquest of Africa is rolling steadily on.[7]

None of this would have been possible whilst Gaddafi was still in power. As founder of the African Union, its biggest donor, and its one-time elected Chairman, he wielded serious influence on the continent. It was partly thanks to him that the U.S. was forced to establish AFRICOM's HQ in Stuttgart in Germany when it was established in February 2008, rather than in Africa itself; he offered cash and investments to African governments who rejected U.S. requests for bases. Libya under his leadership had an estimated $150 billion of investments in Africa,[8] and the Libyan proposal, backed with £30 billion cash, for an African Union Development Bank would have seriously reduced African financial dependence on the West.[9] In short, Gaddafi's Libya was the single biggest obstacle to AFRICOM penetration of the continent.

Now he has gone, AFRICOM is stepping up its work. The invasions of Iraq and Afghanistan showed the West that wars in which their own citizens get killed are not popular; AFRICOM is designed to ensure that in the coming colonial wars against Africa, it will be Africans who do the fighting and dying, not Westerners. The forces of the African Union are to become integrated into AFRICOM under a U.S.-led chain of command. Gaddafi would never have stood for it; that is why he had to go.

And if you want a vision of Africa under AFRICOM tutelage, look no further than Libya, NATO's model of an African state: condemned to decades of violence and trauma, and utterly incapable of either providing for its people, or contributing to regional or continental independence. The new military colonialism in Africa must not be allowed to advance another inch. ☐

The imperial agenda of the US's 'Africa Command' marches on

Originally published by the Guardian, 14 June 2012

"**THE** less they see of us, the less they will dislike us.*" So remarked Frederick Roberts, British general during the Anglo-Afghan war of 1878-80, ushering in a policy of co-opting Afghan leaders to control their people on the empire's behalf.

"Indirect rule", as it was called, was long considered the linchpin of British imperial success, and huge swaths of that empire were conquered, not by British soldiers, but by soldiers recruited elsewhere in the empire. It was always hoped that the dirty work of imperial control could be conducted without spilling too much white man's blood.

It is a lesson that has been re-learned in recent years. The ever-rising western body counts in Iraq and Afghanistan have reminded politicians that colonial wars in which their own soldiers are killed do not win them popularity at home.[1] The hope in both cases is that U.S. and British soldiers can be safely extricated, leaving behind a proxy force to do the killing on our behalf.

And so too in Africa.

To reassert its waning influence on the continent in the face of growing Chinese investment, the U.S. established Africom—the "Africa Command" of the U.S. military—in October 2008.[2] Africom co-ordinates all U.S. military activity in Africa and, according to its mission statement, "contributes to increasing security and stability in Africa—allowing African states and regional organizations to promote democracy, to expand development, to provide for their common defense, and to better serve their people".

However, in more unguarded moments, officials have been more straightforward: Vice Admiral Robert Moeller declared in a conference

The Libyan conflict of 2011 was 'the first war actually commanded by Africom'. Above, 500 lb. bombs are loaded onto a U.S. A-6E Intruder aircraft prior to an air strike on targets in Libya.

in 2008 that Africom was about preserving "the free flow of natural resources from Africa to the global market", and two years later, in a piece in Foreign policy magazine, wrote: "Let there be no mistake. Africom's job is to protect American lives and promote American interests."[3] Through this body, western powers are resorting to the use of military power to win back the leverage once attained through financial monopoly.

The small number of U.S. personnel actually working for Africom—approximately 2,000—belies both the ambition of the project and the threat it poses to genuine African independence. The idea, once again, is that it will not be U.S. or European forces fighting and dying for western interests in the coming colonial wars against Africa, but Africans. The U.S. soldiers employed by Africom are not there to fight, but to direct; the great hope is that the African Union's forces can be subordinated to a chain of command headed by Africom.

Libya was a test case. The first war actually commanded by Africom, it proved remarkably successful—a significant regional power was destroyed without the loss of a single U.S. or European soldier.[4] But the significance of this war for Africom went much deeper than that for, in taking out Muammar Gaddafi, Africom had actually eliminated the project's fiercest adversary.

Gaddafi ended his political life as a dedicated pan-Africanist with a vision of Africa very different from that of the subordinate supplier of cheap labour and raw materials that Africom was created to maintain. He was not only the driving force behind the creation of the African Union in 2002, but had also served as its elected head, and made Libya its biggest financial donor. To the dismay of some of his African colleagues, he used his time as leader to push for a "United States of Africa", with a single currency, single army and single passport.[5] More concretely, Gaddafi's Libya had an estimated $150 billion worth of investment in Africa—often in social infrastructure and development projects—and this largesse bought him many friends, particularly in the smaller nations.[6] As long as Gaddafi retained this level of influence in Africa, Africom was going to founder.

Since his removal, however, the organisation has been rolling full steam ahead. It is no coincidence that within months of the fall of Tripoli—and in the same month as Gaddafi's execution—President Obama announced the deployment of 100 U.S. special forces to four different African countries, including Uganda.[7] Ostensibly to aid the "hunt for Joseph Kony", they are instead training Africans[8] to fight the U.S.'s proxy war in Somalia—where 2,000 more Ugandan soldiers had been sent the previous month.[9]

Fourteen major joint military exercises between Africom and African states are also due to take place this year; and a recent press release from the Africa Partnership Station—Africom's naval training programme—explained that 2013's operations will be moving "away from a training-intensive program" and into the field of "real-world operations".[10]

This is a far cry from the Africa of 2007, which refused to allow Africom a base on African soil, forcing it to establish its headquarters in Stuttgart, Germany. Gaddafi's Libya had served not only as a bulwark against U.S. military designs on the continent, but also as a crucial bridge between black Africa south of the Sahara and Arab Africa in the north. The racism of the new NATO-installed Libyan regime,[11] currently supporting what amounts to a nationwide pogrom against the country's black population, serves to tear down this bridge and push back the prospects for African unity still further.[12]

With Africom on the march and its strongest opponent gone, the African Union now faces the biggest choice in its history: Is it to become a force for regional integration and independence, or merely a conduit for continued Western military aggression against the continent? ☐

A review of Maximilian Forte's new book

'Slouching towards Sirte'

Originally published by Ceasefire magazine, 22 April 2013

THE media has gone very quiet on Libya of late; clearly, liberal imperialists don't like to dwell on their crimes. This is not surprising. The modus operandi of the humanitarian imperialist is not one of informed reflection, but only permanent outrage against leaders of the global South; besides, in the topsy-turvy world of liberal interventionism, the *"failure to act"* is the only crime of which the West is capable. As Forte puts it, their moral code holds that "If we do not act, we should be held responsible for the actions of others. When we do act, we should never be held responsible for our own actions." With Gaddafi dead, the hunt is on for a new hate figure on whom to spew venom (Syria's Bashar al-Assad, Korea's Kim Jong-Un); far more satisfying than actually evaluating our own role in the creation of human misery. This is the colonial mentality of the liberal lynch mob.

For the governments that lead us into war, of course, it makes perfect sense that we do not stop to look back at the last invasion before impatiently demanding the next one—if we realized, for example, that the 1999 bombing of Serbia—the textbook "humanitarian intervention"—actually facilitated the ethnic cleansing of Kosovo it was supposedly designed to prevent, we might not be so ready to demand the same treatment for every other state that falls short of our illusory ideals.

That is why this book is so important. Thoroughly researched and impeccably referenced, it tells the story of the real aims and real consequences of the war on Libya in its historical perspective.

One of the book's accomplishments is its comprehensive demolition of the war's supposed justifications. Forte shows us that

SLOUCHING TOWARDS SIRTE
NATO's War on Libya and Africa

Maximilian Forte

there was no "mass rape" committed by "Gaddafi forces"—as alleged by Susan Rice, Hillary Clinton, Luis Ocampo and others at the time, but later refuted by Amnesty International, the UN and even the U.S. army itself. Despite hysterical media reports, there was no evidence of aerial bombing of protesters, as even CIA chief Robert Gates admitted. Gaddafi had no massacre planned for Benghazi, as had been loudly proclaimed by the leaders of Britain, France and the U.S.A: the Libyan government forces had not carried out massacres against civilian populations in any of the other towns they recaptured from the rebels, and nor had Gaddafi threatened to do so in Benghazi; in a speech that was almost universally misreported in the Western media, he promised no mercy *for those who had taken up arms against the government*, whilst offering amnesty for those who "threw their weapons away", and at no point threatening reprisals against civilians. When the NATO invasion began, French jets actually bombed a small retreating column of Libyan armour on the outskirts of Benghazi, comprising 14 tanks, 20 armoured personnel carriers, and a few trucks and ambulances—nothing like enough to carry out a "genocide" against an entire city, as had been claimed.

Indeed, the whole image of "peaceful protesters being massacred" was turning reality on its head. In fact, Forte notes, rebels "torched police stations, broke into the compounds of security services, attacked government offices and torched vehicles" from the very start, to which the authorities responded with "tear gas, water cannons and rubber bullets—very similar to methods frequently used in Western nations against far more peaceful protests that lacked the element of sedition". Only once the rebels had proceeded to occupy the Benghazi army barracks, loot its weapons, and start using them against government forces did things begin to escalate.

But the most pernicious of the lies that facilitated the Libyan war was the myth of the "African mercenary". Racist pogroms were characteristic of the Libyan rebellion from its very inception, when 50 sub-Saharan African migrants were burnt alive in Al- Bayda on the second day of the insurgency. An Amnesty International report from September 2011 made it clear that this was no isolated incident: "When al-Bayda, Benghazi, Derna, Misrata and other cities first fell under the control of the NTC in February, anti-Gaddafi forces carried out house raids, killings and other violent attacks" against sub-Saharan Africans and black Libyans, and "what we are seeing in western Libya is a very similar pattern to what we have seen in Benghazi and Misrata after those cities fell to the rebels"—arbitrary detention, torture and execution of black people. The "African mercenary" myth was thus created to justify these pogroms, as the Western media near-universally referred to their victims as "mercenaries"—or "alleged mercenaries" in the more circumspect and highbrow outlets—and thus as aggressors and legitimate targets. The myth was completely discredited by both Amnesty International—whose exasperated researcher told a TV interviewer that "We examined this issue in depth and found no evidence: The rebels spread these rumors everywhere [with] terrible consequences for African guest workers"—and by a UN investigation team, who drew similar conclusions—but not until both organisations had already helped perpetuate the lie themselves.

> *Racist pogroms were characteristic of the Libyan rebellion from its very inception, when 50 sub-Saharan African migrants were burnt alive in Al- Bayda on the second day of the insurgency.*

That liberal humanitarians would launch a war of aggression in order to facilitate racist massacres is not as ironic as it might at first seem. Forte writes that "if this was humanitarianism, it could only be so by disqualifying Africans as members of humanity." But such disqualification has been a systematic practice of liberalism from the days of John Locke, through the U.S. war of independence and into the age of nineteenth century imperialism and beyond. Indeed, Forte argues that the barely-veiled "racial fear of mean African bogeymen swamping Libya like zombies" implicit in the "African mercenary" story, was uniquely and precisely formulated to tap into a rich historical vein of

European fantasies about plagues of black mobs. That the myth gained so much traction despite zero evidence, says Forte, "tells us a great deal about the role of racial prejudice and propaganda in mobilizing public opinion in the West and organizing international relations".

Yet the racism of the rebel fighters was not only useful for mobilizing European public opinion—it also played a strategic function, as far as NATO planners were concerned. By bringing to power a virulently anti-black government, the West has ensured that Libya's trajectory as a pan-African state has been brought to a violent end, and that its oil wealth will no longer be used for African development. As Forte succinctly put it, "the goal of U.S. military intervention was to disrupt an emerging pattern of independence and a network of collaboration within Africa that would facilitate increased African self-reliance. This is at odds with the geostrategic and political economic ambitions of extra-continental European powers, namely the U.S."

A large part of the book is dedicated to outlining Libya's role in the creation of the African Union, and its subsequent moves to unify Africa at the economic, political and military levels. This included the investment of billions of petrodollars in industrial development across the continent, the creation of an African communications satellite, and massive financial contributions towards the African Development Bank and the African Monetary Fund—institutions designed specifically to challenge the hegemony of the International Monetary Fund and the World Bank. Gaddafi was passionate about using Libyan oil money to help Africa industrialise and "add value" to its export materials, moving it away from its prescribed role in the global economy as a supplier of cheap raw materials. This was a threat to Western financial and corporate control of African economies, and combined with the rise of Chinese investment, was considered a strategic obstacle to Western domination that had to be removed. As Forte put it, "The U.S., France and the UK could not afford to see allies that they had cultivated, if not installed in power, being slowly pulled from their orbits by Libya, China and other powers". The African Oil Policy initiative Group—a high level U.S. Committee comprising members of Congress, military officers and energy industry lobbyists—noted in 2002 the growing dependence of the U.S. on African oil, and recommended a "new and vigorous focus on U.S. military cooperation in sub-Saharan Africa, to include design of a sub-unified

Black African residents of Libya were largely forced into refugee camps by the rebels' violence against them.

command structure which could produce significant dividends in the protection of U.S. investments". They noted that "failure to address the issue of focusing and maximizing U.S. diplomatic and military command organization...could...act as an inadvertent incentive for U.S. rivals such as China [and] adversaries such as Libya". In other words, with their economic grip on the continent facing serious challenge, the Western world would increasingly have to rely on aggressive militarism in order to maintain its interests.

The recommendations of the committee would be implemented in 2006 with the creation of AFRICOM—the U.S. army's African Command. AFRICOM was conceived as a sort of "School of the Americas' for Africa, designed to train African armies for use as proxy forces for maintaining Western control, with the 2010 U.S. National Security Strategy specifically naming the African Union as one of the regional organisations it sought to co-opt. Libya, however, proved most uncooperative. The leaked U.S. diplomatic cables make it very clear that Libya was viewed by the U.S. as *the* main obstacle to establishing a full muscular U.S. military presence on the African continent, regularly highlighting its "opposition" and "obstruction" to AFRICOM. With Gaddafi still a respected voice within the AU, having served as its elected Chairman in 2009, he wielded significant influence, and used this to spearhead opposition to what he considered the neocolonial aims of the AFRICOM initiative. Meanwhile, Chinese investment in Africa was growing rapidly, from $6 billion in 1999 to $90 billion ten years later, displacing the U.S. as the continent's largest trading partner. The need for a U.S. military presence to cling on to the West's declining influence in Africa was growing ever more urgent. But Africa was not playing ball—and Gaddafi was (rightly) seen as leading the charge.

Fast forward to 2012, and U.S. General Carter Ham, head of AFRICOM, was able to claim that "the conduct of military operations in Libya did afford now the opportunity to establish a military to military relationship with Libya, which did not previously exist". He went on to suggest that a U.S. base would be established in the country (Gaddafi having expelled both the U.S. and British bases shortly after coming to power in 1969), saying that some "assistance" would probably be necessary, in the form of a "military presence". President Obama wasted no time in announcing the deployment of soldiers to four more African countries within weeks of the fall of Tripoli, and AFRICOM announced an unprecedented 14 joint military exercises in Africa for the following year.

Furthermore, NATO's attack had not only destroyed a powerful force for unity and independence in Africa,

> *NATO's attack had not only destroyed a powerful force for unity and independence ... but it had also created the perfect conditions to justify further invasions.*

and a huge obstacle to Western military penetration of the continent, but it had also created the perfect conditions to justify further invasions. The U.S. had previously attempted to argue that its military presence was required in North Africa in order to fight against Al Qaeda; indeed, it had set up the Trans-Saharan Counter Terrorism Programme to this end. But as Muattasim Gaddafi had explained to Hillary Clinton in Washington in 2009, the programme had been rendered redundant by the existing, and highly effective, security strategy of CEN-SAD (the Libyan-led Community of Sahel and Saharan states) and the North African Standby Force. Like a classic protection racket, however, the British, U.S. and French decided that if their protection was not needed, then they would have to create a need for it. The destruction of Libya tore the heart out of the North African security system, flooded the region with weapons and turned Libya into an ungoverned safe haven for violent militias. Now the resulting—and entirely predictable—instability has spread to Mali, the West are using it as an excuse for another war and occupation. In a prescient warning (the book was published before France's recent invasion of Mali), Forte wrote that "intervention begets intervention. More intervention is needed to solve the problems caused by intervention".

The book also exposes the ideology of the "human rights industry" and its role in bringing about the Libyan war. Western liberal humanitarianism, argues Forte, "can only function by first directly or indirectly creating the suffering of others, and by then seeing every hand as an outstretched hand, pleading or welcoming". He exposes the role of groups like Amnesty International and Human Rights Watch, who helped perpetuate some of the worst lies about what was happening in Libya, such as the fictitious "African mercenaries" and "mass rape", and who in the case of Amnesty, "mere days into the uprising and well before it had a chance to ascertain, corroborate or confirm any facts on the ground...began launching public accusations against Libya, the African Union and the UNSC for failing to take action". By calling for an assets freeze on Libya and an arms embargo ("and more actions with each passing day"), Amnesty "thus effectively made itself a party to the conflict"; it had become part of the propaganda war and mythmaking that was designed to facilitate the invasion.

This should not be surprising given Amnesty's history. Forte recalls that their promotion of the infamous "incubator babies" myth that justified the Iraq war of 1991 was later said by many Senators to have influenced their decision to vote for the attack. In the event, the Senate vote was passed by a majority of just six. The 1991 war devastated Iraq, which had barely recovered from the Iran-Iraq war and killed well over 100,000 people, as well as hundreds of thousands more from the diseases that ravaged the country following the deliberate destruction of its water and sewerage systems.

So it should be little surprise that Suzanne Nossel, a State Department official on Hillary Clinton's team, was made Executive

Director of Amnesty-U.S.A in November 2011. In her State Department job, Nossell had played a key role drawing up the UN Human Rights Council resolution against Libya that ultimately formed the basis of Security Council resolution 1973, leading to Libya's bombardment.

Forte also discusses the role of Bouchuiguir, the "human rights activist" who emerges as the Libyan "Curveball". Curveball was the Iraqi "source" who came up with the lies about Saddam's nonexistent "mobile chemical weapons factories" that were used to justify the 2003 Iraq war. Likewise, Bouchuiguir's wildly inflated casualty figures provided the raw material for the hysterical UNHRC resolutions against Libya that set the ball for war rolling. He admitted on camera later that there was no evidence for his claims—but not before 70 NGOs had signed a petition "demanding action" in response to them.

Much has been written elsewhere about the "neo-cons" who became (rightly) hated for their brutally idiotic conceptions of social change. But the liberal humanitarians are perhaps even more contemptible; after all, at least the neo-cons never claimed to be kind, or even driven by anything other than their own self-interest. Yet the liberal humanitarians seem—or at least claim—to be driven by some kind of higher purpose, which makes their constant calls for wars of aggression even more repulsive. Forte puts it brilliantly: "The vision of our humanity that liberal imperialists entertain is one which constructs us as shrieking sacks of emotion. This is the elites' anthropology, one that views us as bags of nerve and muscle: throbbing with outrage, contracting with every story of 'incubator babies', bulging up with animus at the arrest of Gay Girl in Damascus, recoiling at the sound of Viagra-fuelled mass rape. From mass hysteria in twitter to hundreds of thousands signing an online Avaaz petition calling for bombing Libya in the name of human rights, we become nerves of mass reaction....We scream for action via 'social media', thumbs furiously in action on our 'smart' phones. ..Then again, our 'action' merely consists of asking the supremely endowed military establishment to act in our name." This anthropology is of course "accompanied by NATO's implicit sociology: Societies can be remade through a steady course of high altitude bombings and drone strikes."

How exactly Libya has been remade is also discussed. The July 2012 elections in Libya, their very existence trumpeted in Western media as immediately vindicating every act of butchery the war brought about—regardless of whether the parliament being elected was likely to wield any actual influence over the country—saw fewer than half the eligible voting population take part. Even more intriguing were the results of a survey carried out in Libya by Oxford Research International that found that only 13% of Libyans said they wanted democracy within a year's time, and only 25% within five years.

Meanwhile, the new authorities set about persecuting their opponents, real and imagined. Tawergha was emptied of its entire population of around 20,000 black Libyans after militias from Misrata began systematically torching every home and business in the town, with the support of the central government. Former residents now reside in refugee camps where they continue to be hunted down and killed, or in arbitrary detention in makeshift prisons. Meanwhile, candidacy for elections is barred to: workers (a professional qualification is needed); anyone who ever worked in any level of government between 1969 and 2011 (unless they could demonstrate "early and clear" support for the insurrection); anyone with academic study involving Gaddafi's Green book; and anyone who ever received any monetary benefit from Gaddafi. A constitutional lawyer noted these restrictions would disqualify three-fourths of the Libyan population. Other new laws banned the spreading of "news reports, rumours or propaganda" that could "cause any damage to the state", with penalties of up to life in prison; and prison for anyone spreading information that "could weaken the citizens' morale" or for anyone who "attacks the February 17 revolution, denigrates Islam, the authority of the state or its institutions". This is the new Libya for which the human rights imperialists and their allies lobbied, killed and tortured so hard.

"The next time empire comes knocking in the name of human rights", concludes Forte, "please be found standing idly by".

This book is a must-read for anyone seriously interested in understanding the motives and consequences of the West's onslaught against Libya and African development. □

Libya, liberalism and the armies of the global South

When are humans not human?

Originally published in the Morning Star, 15 August 2012

EVER since its inception in the seventeenth century, liberalism has been a wholly hypocritical ideology, based not on the principle of the indivisibility of humanity, as its adherents claim, but on precisely the opposite—endlessly redefined categories of exclusion. The founder of modern Liberalism, John Locke, formulated the principles of England's '"Glorious Revolution" of 1688, supposedly entrenching the "natural rights" to "life, liberty and property" with which he believed all humans were born. All that is, except Catholics—whose support for the wrong side in the English civil war was to be the pretext for continuing to deny their basic rights for the next 150 years—and Africans, who, by a simple logical trick, were simply categorised by Locke as not human at all.[1]

Ever since then, Liberalism's so-called "universal" human rights have been anything but; Locke's exceptions have become the rule. A century after the "Glorious Revolution", the U.S.'s founding fathers followed up their victory in the war against English rule by enshrining basic liberal values into their new constitution. This time "life, liberty and the pursuit of happiness" were the human rights to which all were entitled. Following Locke, the continuation of slavery presented no contradiction here—Africans were simply written off as not fully human—only three fifths human, in fact—and thus exempt from the "natural rights" inherent to all men.

In our times, the ideological somersault has been slightly more subtle than the simple demonization of Africans or Catholics. The people now deemed unworthy of even the most basic human right—the right to life—are soldiers. This is the barbaric flipside of all the feigned concern for civilians in Syria and Libya that has been pouring out of the mouths of our politicians and media pundits for the past year.

This focus on civilians is intentionally designed to hide the horrific reality of what has actually been taking place—the systematic strafing and murder of Libyan and Syrian troops in their tens of thousands—troops who have never invaded another country, many of whom have not even been involved in the retaking of rebel cities, and many still in their teens.

Of course, civilians were killed by NATO as well—and not just mistakenly either. Defence Secretary Liam Fox effectively admitted that Gaddafi's baby grandchildren (all aged between six months and two years), blown to pieces by NATO in late April last year, were deliberately targeted as part of a strategy to "put psychological pressure on Gadaffi".[2] But these deaths were at least reported *as deaths* in the Western media, and briefly caused some controversy. Likewise, the Guardian reported on its front page the news that NATO had deliberately left 61 migrants to die of thirst in the Mediterranean,[3] some of the 1500 civilians estimated to have died there whilst attempting to flee NATO's war.[4]

Deaths of Libyan soldiers, however, were *never* reported by Western news corporations as deaths of human beings. At best, there were veiled references to the "degrading of Gaddafi's military capability" or of "Gaddafi's capacity to attack civilians". The latter is particularly odious. Soldiers have become, it seems, not human beings—people with lives, feelings and families—but merely the "capacity to attack civilians".

Barely six weeks into the invasion, British officials were already boasting that Gaddafi had only "around 30 per cent of his ground forces capability remaining". Having estimated an initial "capacity" of 50,000, the official is apparently attributing to NATO the destruction of around 35,000 people.

The ideological focus on civilians and no one else does not take much decoding. It is clearly an exclusionary category—civilians are precisely *not-soldiers*. Therefore the statement "when we bomb Libya, we are going to save civilians" might be a more palatable way of saying "we are going to incinerate all 50,000 members of the Libyan armed forces", but essentially means exactly the same thing: No soldiers will be spared.

Of course, the massacre of male soldiers also helped to facilitate the slaughter of NATO's beloved civilians as well, as women and children were left—and remain—even more vulnerable to the rebel army's rapes and murders after the killing of their husbands and fathers.[5]

We need to challenge this rhetoric about civilian lives, as if no one and nothing else is important. The obsessive focus not only wilfully obscures the massacres of Libyan soldiers, but also justifies the destruction of their economy,[6] infrastructure,[7] telecommunications networks,[8] water supply[9]... once we accept the logic that only civilian lives are important, literally every other possible target becomes fair game.

Of course, when British soldiers get killed, the euphemisms end. When the Taliban "degrade" the British army's "capacity to attack civilians", this is not how it appears in the headlines. British soldiers have names, faces, families, and of course, a just cause. Soldiers of the occupying army are always human, no matter what atrocities they have taken part in; Libyan soldiers are never human—even if they have never fired a shot in their life.

In Syria, the redefining of the English language has become even more tortuous. Until recently, the Western press rarely admitted that the SAS-trained[10] and CIA-funded[11] death squads[12] even had weapons, let alone that they were using them to wage war against any and all supporters of Syria's secular state.[13] Armed men using brutal sectarian violence were instantly whitewashed to become "peaceful protesters" unjustly victimised by the Syrian army.[14] Death figures were reported as if any and all casualties were "civilians" killed by "Assad's forces". Thus, whilst in Libya, soldiers' deaths did not "count", in Syria it is even worse—police and soldiers' deaths *are* counted—not as victims of the West's proxies who actually killed them, but as victims of themselves, of the Syrian state. Even the heavily anti-government Syrian Observatory for Human Rights admits that well over 5000 Syrian soldiers and police have been killed by rebels,[15] with massacres of 80-100 at a time not uncommon.[16] But Western reporting tends to lump these deaths together with figures of rebels killed to produce an overall death rate it attributes solely to the Syrian government. Thus are statistics used to demonise the murdered and build support for their killers.

This dehumanisation of soldiers should come as no surprise. British soldiers too—lionised by politicians and media once dead—are treated as thoroughly expendable whilst alive. The institutionalised bullying—and probable murder—at the Deepcut barracks,[17] the lack of effective post-tour emotional support,[18] and the massive presence of former soldiers amongst the growing army of Britain's homeless are all indicative of a ruling class that treats even its own soldiers with contempt.[19] Many of the RAF crews who carried out the slaughter of the Libyan army actually returned home to find themselves being made redundant.[20] Empire has no loyalty to its servants. Indeed, last year, a judgement by the highest court in the land ruled that British soldiers were in fact *officially* not human—or at least, not covered by the Human Rights Act—after privates were forced by their superior officers into harsh conditions that eventually killed them.[21]

Despite this shoddy treatment of British soldiers, however, it remains the armies of the global South who are the primary targets of demonization and total destruction. The new ideological focus on civilians is just a new disguise for Liberalism's age-old racism, with a little twist to make it more politically correct. In the nineteenth century, non-white peoples were portrayed as subhuman. Today's humanitarian crusaders claim to love those peoples, of course: It's just their armies—their only source of protection—that they want to destroy. ☐

Part Five
Syria—War by Proxy

The West's greatest fear is a peaceful resolution

Originally published by Al-Ahram Weekly, 3 May 2012

THE strategy was simple, clear, tried and tested. It had been used successfully not only against Libya, but also Kosovo (in 1999), and was rapidly under way in Syria. It was to run as follows: train proxies to launch armed provocations; label the state's response to these provocations as genocide; intimidate the UN Security Council—or at least NATO—into agreeing that "something must be done"; incinerate the entire army and any other resistance with fragmentation bombs and Hellfire missiles; and finally install a weak, compliant government to sign off new contracts and alliances drawn up in London, Paris and Washington, whilst the country tears itself apart. Result: the heart torn out of the "axis of resistance" between Iran, Syria and Hezbollah, leaving Iran isolated and the West with a free hand to attack the Islamic republic without fear of regional repercussions.

This was to be Syria's fate, drawn up years ago in the high level planning committees of U.S., British and French defence departments and intelligence services. But this time, unlike in Libya, it has not all gone according to plan.

First, there was Russia and China's veto of the "regime change" resolution at the UN Security Council in October 2011, followed by a second veto the following February. This meant that any NATO attack on Syria would be denied the figleaf of UN approval, and seen instead as a unilateral act of aggression—not just against Syria, but potentially against China and Russia as well. Vicious and reckless as they are, even Cameron, Sarkozy and Obama do not necessarily have the stomach for *that* kind of a fight. That left the burden of destroying the Syrian state to NATO's proxy forces on the ground, the "Free

Syria Army"—a collection of domestic and (increasingly) foreign rival armed militias, mostly ultra-sectarian Salafi extremists, along with a smattering of defectors and Western special forces.

However, this army was not created to actually defeat the Syrian state; that was always supposed to be NATO's job. As in Libya, the role of the militias was simply to provoke reprisals from the state in order to justify a NATO blitzkrieg. Left to their own devices, they have no chance of gaining power militarily, as many in the opposition realise. "We don't believe the Free Syrian Army is a project that can help the Syrian revolution," said the leader of the internal peaceful Syrian resistance movement, Haytham Al-Manna, recently, "we don't have an example where an armed struggle against a dictatorial regime won." Of course, one could cite Cuba, South Vietnam, and many others; but what is certainly true is that internal armed struggle alone has never succeeded when the government is the only single party in the struggle with any significant mass support—such as in Syria.

This reality was brutally driven home in early March, in the decisive battle for the Baba Amr district of Homs. This was supposedly one of the Free Syrian Army's strongholds, yet they were roundly defeated, leaving them facing the prospect of similar defeats in their last few remaining territories as well. The opposition are increasingly aware that their best chance of meaningful change is not through a military fight that they will almost certainly lose—and which will get them killed in the process, along with their support and credibility—but through negotiations and participation in the reform process and dialogue which the government has offered.

This prospect—of an end to the civil war, and a negotiated peace which brings about a reform process without destabilising the country—has led to desperation amongst the imperial powers. Despite their claims to the contrary, a stable Syrian-led process is the last thing they want, as it leaves open the possibility of Syria remaining a strong, independent, anti-imperialist state—exactly the possibility they had sought to eliminate.

Hence, within days of Kofi Annan's peace plan gaining a positive response from both sides in late March, the imperial powers openly pledged, for the first time, millions of dollars for the Free Syrian Army: for military equipment, to provide salaries to its soldiers, and to bribe government forces to defect. In other words, terrified that the civil war is starting to die down, they are setting about institutionalising it. If violent regime change is starting to look unlikely, the hope instead is to keep the country weak and on its knees by keeping its energy sucked into civil war.

At the risk of making the Syrian National Council appear even more out of touch with ordinary Syrians than it does already, its Western backers have increased the pressure for them to fall into line with this strategy, leading to open calls from the SNC leader-

PHOTO: UN PHOTO/JEAN-MARC FERRÉ

The West's allies responded to the Kofi Annan's peace plan by pouring millions into FSA coffers

ship for both the full scale arming of the rebellion, and for aerial bombardment from the West. This has caused huge rifts in the organisation, with three leading members defecting last month, because they did not want to be "accomplices to the massacre of the Syrian people through delaying, cheating, lies, one-upmanship and monopolisation of decision-making." The SNC, according to one of the three, Kamal al-Labwani, was "linked to foreign agendas which aim to prolong the battle while waiting ... for the country to be dragged into a civil war".

This month one of the very few SNC leaders actually based in Syria, Riad Turk, called on the opposition to accept the Annan peace plan, "stop the bloodshed" and enter dialogue with the government—a call not echoed by his fellow SNC colleagues abroad. Likewise, the main peaceful opposition grouping based within Syria—the National Coordinating Committee—has fallen out with the SNC over the latters' increasingly belligerent role as a mouthpiece of foreign powers. NCC leader Haytham Al-Manna spoke out publicly against the Free Syrian Army recently, saying, "The militarization of the Syrian revolution signifies the death of the internal revolution...We know that the Turkish government plays an important role in the political decisions of the Free Syrian Army. We don't believe that an armed group can be on Turkish territory and remain independent of Turkish decisions."

So there is a growing perception, even amongst the Syrian opposition movement itself, that both the Free Syrian Army and the Syrian National Council are working in the interests of foreign powers to prolong a damaging civil war.

Western policy makers are playing a dangerous game. Short of a NATO attack, their best option for the destabilisation and emasculation of Syria is to ensure that the ceasefire fails and the fighting continues. To this end, they are encouraging their proxy militias to step up their provocations; the purpose of Clinton and Juppe's statements about "other measures" still being on the table is to keep the idea of a NATO attack alive in the heads of the rebels so that they continue to fight. Indeed, many more foreign fighters have been shipped into the country in recent weeks according to the Washington Post, and have launched devastating bomb attacks in Damascus and Aleppo.[1] U.S. ambassador to Syria, Robert Ford is a protégé of John Negroponte, who organised contra death squads to destabilise Nicaragua in the 1980s; he will almost certainly have been organising similar groups in Syria during his time there last year, for similar purposes.

Nevertheless, the destabilisation agenda is not going according to plan. The internal opposition are becoming increasingly frustrated with the way things are progressing, and a clear split is emerging between those based outside the country, happy to see Syria consigned to oblivion in order to please their paymasters and further their careers, and those who actually have to live with the consequences. The reckless attacks of the armed militias are increasingly alienating even those who once had some sympathy for them, especially as their foreign membership and direction is exposed ever more clearly. Having been proven decisively unable to win and hold territory, these militias are turning to hit-and-run guerrilla tactics. But the guerrilla, as Mao put it, is like a fish, which can only survive in a sea of popular support. And that sea is rapidly drying up. ☐

The Syrian National Initiative

A fig leaf for invasion?

Originally published by Pravda, 22 November 2012

THE formation of the Syrian National Initiative (SNI) was announced last week with much fanfare, replacing the discredited Syrian National Council as the latest front organization for the ongoing war against the Syrian state. Naturally, it was formed in Qatar. As a leading conduit for Western arms, funding and propaganda in the region, the choice of venue was ideally suited to spell out the imperial nature of the operation to anyone who might have missed it.

The timing was as indicative as the venue. Hillary Clinton's outburst that the Syrian National Council was no longer fit for purpose and that the Syrian opposition needed a "more inclusive" body if it wanted greater Western support, was made on October 31. The plan for the Syrian National Initiative was presented two days later by Riad Seif, having been "developed with the help of the U.S. State Department", according to the Carnegie Endowment website. Seif, according to the same website, is a "good friend" of former U.S. ambassador to Syria Robert Ford, himself a protégé of John Negroponte, who ran the Central American death squads out of the U.S. Embassy in Honduras in the 1980s. David Cameron then headed to the region, announcing on November 7, in the arrogance typical of his class, that the Western powers had an opportunity to "shape the opposition" in Syria. Various self-styled opposition spokesmen and figureheads met with U.S., British, French and Turkish officials in Doha the following day, and three days later the Syrian National Initiative was born.

Whatever this new "opposition bloc" is, it is certainly not the "sole representative of the Syrian people", as has now been claimed by France, Turkey and the Gulf states. A referendum in February

The Syrian National Intiative was shaped in Western capitals.

of this year saw 89% of voters support a new Syrian constitution which commits the government to far-reaching political reforms, including the end of the one-party state; and opinion polls conducted by Yougov last year suggested that 55% of Syrians inside Syria (as opposed to the wealthy emigres who tend to monopolise Western media coverage) want Assad to remain as President. Indeed, a Free Syrian Army commander in Syria's second biggest city Aleppo recently admitted that 70% of the population of the city support Assad, and that "it has always been that way".

The SNI cannot even claim to be the legitimate representative of the Syrian *opposition;* i.e. of those Syrians who want to see Assad deposed. The National Coordination Committee, comprising most of the leftist opposition to Assad, and who are opposed to Western intervention and the militarization of the conflict, have wisely not endorsed the project; and one opposition activist told Reuters that "The people inside Syria don't see in the initiative a national vision. They see it as a way to undermine the revolution". Even amongst the groups actually involved, many are clearly only there because they do not want to miss out on any Western money and weapons that may be distributed, rather than out of any commitment to its aims, or unity of purpose with other members. Even the Muslim Brotherhood, the largest political entity amongst the Syrian armed opposition, were vociferous in their opposition to the colonial nature of the initiative, with their spokesman Zuhair Salim initially claiming there was little difference between Hillary Clinton's statement and the Balfour Declaration—before jumping on the bandwagon a few days later nonetheless.

Clearly, this grouping of disparate rivals and factions bound together solely by their opportunism suggests a coalition that is likely to be not only unstable, but dysfunctional. Fearing this, almost all of the real issues were left undiscussed at the Doha conference. As Professor Amr al-Azm has put it, "there are few details regarding the structure of the new coalition, or the mechanisms for decision-making within it. Nor is there a timeline for achieving its political goals in place. This all points to a clear lack of strategy and planning on the part of those who put this coalition together and those currently leading it".

But none of this matters to the instigators of the group. Cameron and Clinton have cobbled this group together for one reason and one reason only—to provide a figleaf of legitimacy for the ramping up of their proxy war against Syria; a war they are still hoping to take all the way to an all out British-French-U.S. bombardment.

A massive escalation is clearly being planned in London and Washington. U.S. and Turkish officials have been speaking about placing U.S. Patriot missiles on the Syrian-Turkish border; British general David Richards said on Sunday (November 11) that the RAF are preparing for a Syrian mission this winter; and reports are now emerging that Free Syrian Army troops—with SAS support—have been stepping up attacks on Syrian air defense systems over recent months. Without air support, the rebels cannot win; any illusions otherwise were dashed by the dismal failures of the rebel offensives in July and August. What has been holding the West back so far has been two things: Chinese and Russian intransigence at the UN Security Council, and the U.S. President's unwillingness to get embroiled in a new war during an election campaign.

The British government were quickest off the mark, their statements that they would now be dealing directly with Syrian armed groups being issued literally within hours of Obama's victory on November 7th; as military analyst Shashank Joshi put it, "With the re-election of Obama, what you have is a strong confidence on the British side that the U.S. administration will be engaged more on Syria from the get-go". With the failure of all attempts to bully China and Russia into acquiescence, plan B is now underway: bypassing the UN Security Council altogether, and attempting to find some alternative legal justification for invasion, however flimsy. Indeed, Phillip Hammond, British Defence Minister, told Andrew Marr last Sunday that his department had effectively been ordered to come up with precisely such a pretext: *"At the moment we don't have a legal basis for delivering military assistance to the rebels. This is something the Prime Minster keeps asking us to test—the legal position, the practical military position, and we will continue to look at all options."*

This is where the Syrian National Initiative comes in. The hope is that they will serve as the legal figleaf for the coming onslaught: If they are the legitimate representatives of the Syrians, the argument will go, and they invite us into their country, then it is not really an invasion—and therefore, not illegal. It is nonsense, of course—but the powers who argued that the WMD gossip of an Iraqi taxi driver constituted a legal basis for the war on Iraq are clearly beyond shame in such matters. □

War on Syria means war on Palestine

Originally published by the Independent, 20 November 2012

WITH OVER 100 now reported killed by Israeli airstrikes, and a further 700 injured, the attack on Gaza is already starting to resemble the 2008-2009 "Operation Cast Lead" massacre.[1] A ground invasion is feared, and Israeli politicians are again trotting out the usual Zionist crowd-pleasers about the need to "bomb Gaza back to the Middle Ages" (Deputy Prime Minister Eli Yishai) and "flatten all of Gaza" (Ariel Sharon's son Gilad).[2]

Yet the regional situation today is very different to what it was back then. In 2009, the "resistance axis" of Iran, Syria, Hezbollah and Hamas was strong, and Iran took concrete steps to provide military supplies to Hamas at a time when the best any other states had to offer was impotent—and generally hypocritical—'"condemnation". As intelligence analysts Stratfor have noted, where "the rest of the region largely avoided direct involvement.... Iran was the exception.

"While the Arab regimes ostracized Hamas, Iran worked to sustain the group in its fight". The report elaborates: "In early January 2009, in the midst of Operation Cast Lead, Israel learned that Iran was allegedly planning to deliver 120 tons of arms and explosives to Gaza, including anti-tank guided missiles and Iranian-made Fajr-3 rockets with a 40-kilometer (25-mile) range and 45-kilogram (99-pound) warhead... The long-range Fajr rocket attacks targeting Tel Aviv and Jerusalem in the current conflict are a testament to Iran's continued effort".[3]

ISOLATED

Despite having distanced themselves from the "resistance axis" recently, moving their headquarters out of Damascus and voicing support for the anti-government militias in Syria, Hamas continue to rely on Iranian weapons as their most effective response to Israeli aggression. Indeed, it is precisely these Iranian weapons—the Fajr-5 missiles—that are causing such unprecedented disruptions in Israel, having reached the suburbs of Tel Aviv and forcing the city's residents into bomb shelters for the first time since 1991. Israelis are not used to their military operations having such a direct impact on their own lives, and it is this aspect of the conflict that has led to, in what is surely a first for Israel,[4] overwhelming Israeli *opposition* to a ground invasion of Gaza, with less than a third supporting such a move.[5]

Nevertheless, the Palestinians, whilst well-equipped, are in some ways more isolated than ever. Whilst on the face of it, the rise of the Muslim Brotherhood across the region in the wake of the "Arab Spring" should have been good news for Hamas—who are, after all, an offshoot of the Brotherhood themselves—the seeming descent of the Arab Spring into a sectarian conflict directed against the region's Shia Muslims has actually served to disempower Hamas' allies, and thus leave Gaza more vulnerable to precisely the attack it is now enduring.[6] More specifically, the ongoing destruction of Syria under the onslaught of armed gangs trained and sponsored by the West and its allies, has crippled a key Palestinian ally, and thus encouraged Israel to believe it can attack with impunity.

As Hezbollah leader Nasrallah ("the smartest guy in the Middle East", according to former U.S. Deputy Secretary of State Richard Armitage) noted in a speech last week, "Israel is taking advantage of the turmoil in Syria in its onslaught against Gaza. Today's aggression is happening in a different context from 2008. In 2008, the Resistance Axis was more capable of extending support to Gaza and the resistance there and this was the case before 2008 and after 2008 and we can see the results of this on the ground today. One of the supply lines to Gaza has now been cut and that is Syria. It can no longer provide logistical support, although it can still take a political stand.

EMBATTLED

Israel is taking advantage of the fighting in Syria, of the reversal of priorities, of the transformation of enemies into friends and friends into enemies. It sees this as a good opportunity to restore its deterrence and to strike at missile capabilities in Gaza, which Israel

is aware will be hard to replace in light of the situation in Syria."
Indeed, with the sectarian attacks taking place in Syria spilling over
into Lebanon, Hezbollah itself is similarly in little position to lend the
type of support to Gaza that it did in 2006, for example, by opening
a second front in response to Israeli shelling of Palestinians. Stratfor again: "Hezbollah will likely be extremely cautious in deciding
whether to participate in this war".

The group's fate is linked to that of the embattled
regime of Syrian President Bashar al Assad; should Syria frac-
ture along sectarian lines, Lebanon is likely to descend into
civil war, and Hezbollah will have to conserve its strength and
resources for a battle at home against its sectarian rivals."[7]
If Syria does fall, therefore, we can expect to see far more Israeli
massacres of the type now currently under way. Not only will Syria
be knocked out of the "resistance axis" altogether, and Hezbollah left
without a supply line from Iran, but Iran itself will be left isolated
and less able to provide the Gazans with the missiles that currently
provide their only effective deterrent to a renewed Israeli occupation.
This goes some way to explaining why the Israelis have been so
supportive of the Syrian rebels, with Peres and Barak both throwing
their weight behind the militias. Syria's support for Hezbollah, and
the link it provides to Iran, has been a key obstacle to Israel's ability
to attack the Palestinians with impunity, and therefore to its ability to
unilaterally impose a final settlement on Palestine. For now, the main
obstacle to the Israeli diktat remains the Fajr-5. □

The British parliament only likes to attack the weak

Originally published by the Asia Times, 6 September 2013

THE House of Commons vote against attacking Syria last Thursday has been widely hailed as unprecedented in modern times. This is the same House that has voted, with huge majorities, for military aggression against Serbia, Iraq, Afghanistan, and Libya—the last in this very parliament—with devastating consequences. It is the same House that has never opposed Britain's role in hugely destructive sanctions on Iran,[1] North Korea[2] and Iraq:[3] sanctions known, and arguably designed, to inflict pain on the civilian populations, and reaching genocidal proportions in the last case according to two high level UN officials.[4] It is the same House that routinely votes through legislation not only allowing people to be detained without charge, but now even stripped of their citizenship so they can be drone blitzed without government embarrassment.[5] Indeed, a case of parliament vetoing military action proposed by the government is so rare that newspapers have reminded us that you have to go back as far as 1782 to find another example; in that case Lord North's plea, at the behest of George III, to continue fighting the American independence movement even after the disastrous and pivotal defeat at Yorktown.

What has happened? What has changed Parliament's mind? Why is it suddenly acting so seemingly out of character? Various explanations have emerged in the British press. For many mainstream newspapers, the issue has been reduced to a technical, bureaucratic issue of "party mismanagement" by David Cameron and his whips—he did not work hard enough to get MPs, and in some cases even government ministers, back from their holidays in time for the vote, or to get cross-party consensus, or to make concessions to his rebellious backbenchers. Others say it was all down to Ed Miliband cynically using the Tory split for party advantage. All this may be true, but it still begs the questions of why the Tories were so split on the issue, and why the vote was going to be so close in the first place? All other votes of this nature have been anything but close; even the celebrated "backbench rebellion" over the Iraq war did not prevent that motion breezing through with a comfortable majority of well over 250.

Much of the anti-war movement are congratulating themselves for the great "victory". Andrew Murray of the Stop the War Coalition wrote in the Guardian that "the sustained mass pressure of the anti-war movement has undoubtedly been a decisive factor" (adding that "Ed Miliband deserves a measure of credit too, of course.")[6] Really? Can we really say that the anti-war movement has exercised "sustained pressure" on the government on this issue? The greatest "anti-war" pressure, surely, came at the time of the Iraq war, since when the movement—at least in terms of numbers participating in any obvious, visible form of collective protest—has collapsed. Indeed, the Coalition itself held its first significant national demonstration against war on Syria only *after* the parliamentary vote had taken place; do its organisers really think that the mere threat of the impending demonstration was what altered lawmakers' opinions? Public opinion has continued to side with the general anti-war sentiment of the movement, undoubtedly, but public opinion alone does not equal "sustained pressure".

Elsewhere the parliamentary vote has been attributed to the lack of evidence that Assad's government were responsible for the attack. Many MPs argued in last week's debate that the experience of being "misled" over Iraq meant that the "bar has now been raised" in terms of the quality of evidence they now demand before supporting military action. Other explanations for the vote's outcome include the idea of "war fatigue" (implied by John Kerry[7]), or of some kind of sudden, road-away-from-Damascus conversion to the sanctity of "public opinion": "MPs can read opinion polls" pointed out the Independent's John Rentoul, as if they had been unable to do so hitherto, and as if the British public ever voted according to foreign policy preferences anyway.

These explanations all have their appeal, no doubt. They add up to a general explanation that parliament has now "learned the

Based on similar lies, the U.S. and UK invaded and occupied Iraq for years, leaving one in three Iraqis dead, wounded or refugees.

lessons" of Iraq, that it can no longer be relied upon to support war in the Middle East in the face of public opinion, on the basis of flimsy evidence, and without regard to the generally-disastrous humanitarian consequences.

This argument might seem plausible if not for one almighty spanner in the logical works. Libya. Two and a half years ago, this same House of Commons voted—by 544 to 13 no less—to support the bombing of Libya in a war which ultimately resulted in the total destruction of the Libyan state, and thus condemned the country to instability and violence for decades to come. Many of the arguments used about Syria now would have equally—if not more so—applied to Libya then. Take the issue of evidence. The momentum for war against Libya, as Thomas Mountain has discussed, was built up primarily on the basis of four major lies.[8] The most important, of course, was that Gaddafi was on the verge of committing a massacre against thousands of innocent civilians—half a million, the Guardian reported—in Benghazi.[9] Yet the evidence for this assertion was even flimsier than the chemical weapons case against Assad, resting solely on one decontextualised extract from a single, badly translated speech by Gaddafi, where he threatened "no mercy" against rebels. He specifically outlined what he meant by rebels—those who had taken up arms against the government and had rejected the government's offer of amnesty should they give themselves up—yet, strangely, the mainstream media chose not to pick up either this caveat or the amnesty offer.[10] As Hugh Roberts of the International Crisis Group has pointed out, the Libyan army's retaking of other rebel-held territories earlier in the uprising had not once resulted in massacres against civilians, and neither had his response to other rebellions at any other time during his forty two years in power: "In retaking the towns that the uprising had briefly wrested from the government's control, Gaddafi's forces had committed no massacres at all; the fighting had been bitter and bloody, but there had been nothing remotely resembling the slaughter at Srebrenica, let alone in Rwanda…[and yet] what was decided was to declare Gaddafi guilty in advance of a massacre of defenceless civilians and instigate the process of destroying his regime and him (and his family) by way of punishment of a crime he was yet to commit, and actually unlikely to commit, and to persist with this process despite his repeated offers to suspend military action". Yet Parliament had been led to believe that Gaddafi had *already* slaughtered at least 6,000 innocent protesters in Benghazi, a number plucked out of the sky by Libyan opposition members,[11] re-tweeted, and then reported as "news" across the globe.[12] Comprehensive research by Amnesty International later revealed the true pre-NATO death toll in Benghazi to be 110—including armed rebels as well as government forces killed by the rebels.[13] Further allegations referred to Gaddafi's use of "African mercenaries" and employment of mass rape as a tactic, "backed up" by re-tweeted opposition claims, "unconfirmed eyewitness reports" and even, bizarrely, Youtube footage of yellow-helmeted construction workers supposedly providing proof of "mercenaries".[14] Both claims were later comprehensively demolished by both Amnesty International and UN investigation teams.[15]

Parliament, however, seems to have had no problem supporting that particular war on the basis of zero credible evidence; indeed

> *Comprehensive research by Amnesty International later revealed the true pre-NATO death toll in Benghazi to be 110—including armed rebels as well as government forces killed by the rebels.*

the word "evidence" was used only three times during the six hour debate that preceded the Libya vote, compared to 112 uses in the six hour debate on Syria last week. So why the sudden concern with evidence where no such concern existed the last time around? Would a parliament that was so eager to destroy Libya on the "evidence" of retweeted gossip and Youtube pictures of people in yellow hats really be unwilling to launch a limited strike on the basis of its own intelligence reports? That idea in itself defies belief as much as anything Tony Blair ever came out with. What seems rather more likely is that MPs were just using the "lack of evidence" issue as a means of hiding the real reasons behind their opposition.

The major difference between Syria now and Libya then is not, in fact, one of evidence, mass pressure, or "war fatigue", but one of strength. Parliament has not changed its ways, it is acting now, just as it was in 2011, 2003 and, indeed, 1782, according to a very consistent principle—wars of choice should only be waged against the weak and isolated. Libya and Iraq were both of these things; Syria is neither. Libya and Iraq had both subjected themselves to comprehensive disarmament programmes prior to being attacked, and both were without strong powerful allies willing to defend them. For Joan Smith, one of the pundits dismayed by the outcome of last week's vote, there is somehow "a massive irony here: We went to war against a tyrant who turned out no longer to have weapons of mass destruction but won't consider limited air strikes against one who has used them in recent days".[16] In fact, there is no irony at all. Leaving aside her credulity over British and U.S. claims to possess secret classified evidence of Assad's guilt, the point is that it is—by definition—much safer to attack countries without an effective deterrent; that is not irony, that is the defining feature of the cowardly brutality that has become such a hallmark of Western behaviour in the Middle East to all those with eyes to see it.

Again, a comparison of the two Commons debates—Syria and Libya, both six hours long—is instructive. The words "consequence" and "consequences" were used twice as much about Syria than about Libya (72 times compared to 35), while the words "escalate" and "escalation" were used eight times as often (33 times compared to just 4). "Retaliate" and "retaliation" were used nine times regarding Syria, compared to just once with Libya. Indeed, doubts concerning the "risk of escalation" were made so frequently during the Syria debate that they were the first issue Nick Clegg attempted to address in his summing up.

This begs the question—exactly what "consequences", "escalation" and "retaliation" is it that MPs are suddenly so worried about? After all, the Libya conflict certainly "escalated", and in fact ended up destroying the security framework of the whole of North Africa. The country now functions as a safe haven and training ground for death squads and gangster elements from across the region, with recent attacks on Algeria and Mali merely the most obvious immediate results. Yet none of this seems to register—either then or now—as much of a concern in the House of Commons. Could this be because the destabilisation of North Africa poses no threat to the projection of British power—and, indeed, fits in rather nicely with Anglo-American plans to weaken Algeria and militarise West Africa? MPs' fears of "escalation", then, cannot be taken to mean a fear of escalation of violence in the region *per se*, but an escalation of violence *directed against Britain, its allies and its interests* in the region. And why would they fear such an escalation in this case? Because of the military power of Syria and her allies. Michael Meacher, Labour MP, stated it clearly: "Let us not forget that Syria is no Libya. It is far stronger than Libya, with far more disciplined and larger armed forces, and it is still powerfully backed and reinforced by Russia."

His point is backed up by the assessments of various military personnel, such as this anonymous U.S. officer quoted in the Washington Post: "I can't believe the president is even considering it. We have been fighting the last ten years a counterinsurgency war. Syria has modern weaponry. We would have to retrain for a conventional war".[17] James Mattis, former head of U.S. Central Command, who oversaw planning for potential U.S. military action in Syria, concurs: "If Americans take ownership of this, this is going to be a full-throated, very, very serious war". Jack Straw, in the parliamentary debate, noted that General Dempsey, chairman of the Joint Chiefs of Staff of the U.S. armed forces, had already "spelt out that fully to [degrade Syria's chemical weapons capability] would involve hundreds of ships and aircraft and thousands of ground troops, at a cost of $1 billion per month". Syria's strength is also underlined by Robert Kaplan in an article questioning comparisons between a war against Syria and the

78 day NATO bombing of Serbia in 1999: "Syria has a population ten times the size of Kosovo's in 1999. Because everything in Syria is on a much vaster scale, deciding the outcome by military means could be that much harder".[18] He also recognises that, whilst terrorising the population would be the clear aim of any aerial bombing campaign, the 30 months of terror bombing[19] *already* suffered by Syrians at the hands of British-backed death squads may have somewhat hardened them against any additional terror from the skies: "The Kosovo war inflicted significant pain on Serbian civilians through airstrikes, but the Syrian population has already been pummelled by a brutal war for two years now, and so it is problematic whether airstrikes in this case can inflict that much more psychological pain on the parts of the population either still loyal or indifferent to the regime".[20]

As well as Russian support, Kaplan identified Syria's alliance with Iran as another serious obstacle: "The Kosovo war did not engage Iran as this war must. For all of the missiles that America can fire, it does not have operatives on the ground like Iran has. Neither will the United States necessarily have the patience and fortitude to prosecute a lengthy and covert ground-level operation as Iran might for years to come, and already has".

George Friedman writing for global intelligence analysts Stratfor, notes that Russia and Iran "might both retaliate were someone to attack the Syrian regime...If [Obama] strikes, he must prepare for Russian counters...Libya was easy compared to Syria".[21] Likewise, the Jamestown Foundation noted earlier this year that "A stark warning to the West that Tehran would retaliate if Syria was attacked came on January 26 from Ali Akbar Velayati, a close advisor to Iran's Supreme Leader, Ayatollah Ali Khamenei. According to Velayati, Syria is the "resistance front" and any attack on Iran's strongest ally in the region would be considered an attack on Iran".[22] Lebanese scholar Amal Saad-Ghorayeb is more precise: "When the takfiri rebels attacked Lebanese villages and Lebanese civilians inside Syria, Hezbollah's response was to openly engage them in Qusayr. When they staged terrorist attacks in Dahyeh, Nasrallah threatened them with doubling the number of Hezbollah fighters in Syria. It doesn't take a huge leap of the imagination to fathom just how much more of an existential threat an American-Zionist-Arab scheme to destroy the Syrian Army would pose to Hezbollah's resistance and Lebanon's internal security.

And Hezbollah wouldn't even need to retaliate against Israel from Lebanon, but would do so from Syria itself, alongside the Syrian Army and with Iranian military assistance". That Syria's friends were clearly on the minds of MPs last Thursday is illustrated by their references to these allies, with Hezbollah mentioned 11 times, Iran 43 times, and Russia 68 times. Patrick Cockburn in the Independent, put it simply: "In one crucial respect Assad is in a stronger position than Slobodan Milosevic in Serbia, Saddam Hussein in Iraq or Muammar Gaddafi in Libya. These three leaders were internationally isolated, while Assad has powerful and committed foreign allies".[23] This is what has changed parliament's mind; they prefer to fight their wars against the weak and vulnerable.

And what of the argument that the MPs were now finally following public opinion? Certainly the public is much more united over its opposition to attacks on Syria[24] than they were to attacks on Libya,[25] but this still begs the question of *why* does the public so strongly oppose action now, where they did not in 2011? The public, too, fear "escalation"—in other words, they too know that Syria is strong, and supported by powerful allies. As Tory MP Sarah Wollaston put it during the debate, "The country is almost unanimously opposed to unilateral Western military intervention. That is not because we are a nation of appeasers and apologists; it is because the nation rightly has weighed up the risks of such action exploding into a wider military conflict with hundreds of thousands more deaths". This does not mean that MPs are "listening" to public opinion; merely that both are following the same logic—don't attack the strong.

Not that this means that an attack will not take place anyway, or that Britain will not be involved—regardless of parliament's well-founded fears of serious military resistance. The Great Recession facing the global capitalist system today is pushing inexorably towards major war in just the same way as the Great Depressions of 1873-96 and 1929-39 were pushing towards war, and for the same reason—the need to destroy surplus capital and pave the way for a new round of profitable investment. Likewise, the crisis of Western hegemony—the imminent prospect of an end to 500 years of Western military preponderance in the face of a resurgent global South—is leaving "the West" with ever fewer options other than the obliteration of all independent regional powers in order to preserve its dominance.

There is indeed a "red line" in Syria, but it has nothing to do with chemical weapons—the real red line is the prospect of a victory for the Syrian government. This is the scenario which the Franco-Anglo-Saxons will not tolerate without throwing everything they have into the fight, and this is why now, at last, they are seriously contemplating an air campaign—because everything else they have tried has failed. It is far from over yet. □

Part Six
Media War

Reflections on rebellious media

An edited version of this article was originally published in the Morning Star, 12 October 2011.

WHO better to open a conference on "Rebellious Media" than Noam Chomsky? The arch-rebel of U.S. academia and proponent of the "propaganda model" of the media, at 82-years-old he is now not only the best-known but probably also the longest-serving celebrity critic of U.S. foreign policy in the world. And unlike many academics, he is not scared to "get his hands dirty" by discussing—and critiquing—strategy with the resistance movements of which he most definitely considers himself to be a part.

So it should perhaps be no surprise that his talk today focuses on the weaknesses of the Occupy Wall Street movement. Whilst overall, of course, he considers the protest, and its rapid, "wildcat" spread around the U.S., to be a good thing, he is not so enamoured with its public demands. "Here are some of the phrases that are missing from the Occupy Wall Street programme", he explains: "Iraq. Afghanistan. War. Industry. Factory. Women. Healthcare."

But there was another word that was missing—not only from the protesters' programme, but from Chomsky's critique, the questions from his audience, and indeed from almost the entire conference. Libya.

As the conference opened, the Libyan town of Sirte was experiencing its 30th successive day of full scale bombardment and siege from NATO and their Libyan allies, leaving the population "dying from lack of water, medicine and electricity", according to the Telegraph. Into the town's housing blocks, "rebels were pouring rocket after rocket from launchers mounted on pickup trucks" it continued, whilst

PHOTO: YANG GUANG

NATO bombing raids on Libya.

"gunmen assured reporters that there were few families left inside". Indeed, 20,000 are reported to have fled the city. This leaves 80,000 to face the rockets and enforced malnutrition.

John Pilger does touch on this later in the proceedings, in response to a question from the audience: "As we speak", he says, "Sirte is being blasted with iron fragmentation bombs and hellfire missiles in an attack comparable to that on Fallujah". He has been vitriolic in his condemnation of NATO atrocities against Libya ever since his excellent article on the subject, published on April 6, two weeks after NATO began their blitzkrieg and six weeks after the Libyan contras lynched their first group of fifty unarmed African migrant workers. But until then, he—and many others—had been silent. When it was most important to speak out was *before* the invasion, when the die was being cast, when "consent" was being "manufactured" (to use Chomsky's phrase) with lies about ten thousand dead, mass rape, mercenaries and the aerial bombing of demonstrators. As it turned out, none of these were actions perpetrated by Gaddafi's forces, but were the fantasies of NATO and their Libyan allies about what they *themselves* were about to unleash. But neither Pilger nor Chomsky warned of this nor exposed these lies during that crucial phase.

So the question I want, urgently, to discuss at the conference is—what is the role of radical media *during the demonization phase*—the inevitable prelude to any war? I brought it up at every session I went to, and when I did, many people were eager to discuss it. But, sadly, it was never discussed on any of the panels.

Later in the day, Zahera Harb gave an excellent presentation on Hezbollah's media tactics, most effective of which was their use of what they termed "media traps". After the 1996 Israeli bombardment and occupation of Lebanon, Hezbollah devised a new strategy aimed at appealing to the Israeli public. But to do this, they needed to gain credibility. They began by taking professional cameramen, with hi-tech equipment, with them on each of their operations. After an operation, they would then release a press release saying how many Israeli soldiers they had killed and injured. The Israeli government would inevitably issue their own statement denying the story. Hezbollah would then release some grainy, far off footage of the attack in support of their claims, which Israel would again rebuff. Then came the trap. The high quality footage would finally be released, proving that Hezbollah had been telling the truth—and the Israelis lying—all along. They successfully used this tactic no less than four separate times. Harb argued that it played an important role in undermining support for the occupation amongst the Israeli public, and thus in persuading Israel to eventually pull out almost all its forces in 2000.

It occurs to me that we too have been caught in a media trap, albeit an unintentional one of our own making, borne of our own prejudices. Almost all of Gaddafi's claims—of Al Qaeda involvement in the uprising, of systematic racist atrocities carried out by rebel forces, of the rebels being in the pay of foreign interests aiming to destabilise and conquer the country—have been proven correct. And we, including a huge number on the left, have been caught lying—that the uprising was essentially a liberal democratic one, that the rebels were a nonviolent protest movement, that Gaddafi was a genocidal rapist and on and on.

An insight into why so many journalists were so ready to credulously repeat these lies was provided by Andy Williams' presentation on the growing influence of Public Relations companies in the media. His research found that the amount of copy expected from journalists has tripled in recent years, with half of those interviewed reporting less time to properly check facts. As a result, they are becoming increasingly reliant on press releases, often from Public Relations firms working for private companies (and, we can safely assume, for governments, intelligence agencies, and military forces). Of the 2000 articles he analysed, 1 in 5 were wholly plagiarised from press releases, with no additional information whatsoever. A further 1 in 3 relied on press releases for more than half of the copy. Only 1 in 10 contained no obvious "pre-packaged" material. His conclusion was that mainstream journalism was increasingly being reduced to "cutting and pasting press releases"—and therefore increasingly manufactured by political and business elites. In the case of Libya this was absolutely clear, with even easily checkable (dis)information—such as Gaddafi's supposed bombing of parts of Tripoli, easily disproved by a simple visit to the areas in question—being reported as "fact".

Elsewhere, Greg Philo summarised the findings of the Glasgow Media Group's meticulous research into media presentation of the Palestine-Israel conflict. "There are a great range of positions [on the conflict] amongst journalists", he explained, "but when you look at their output, this is not reflected". The reasons are pretty clear; the power of the Israeli lobby, the prejudices of the Murdoch press, and the geostrategic interests of British ruling elites all dictate a heavily pro-Israeli bias.   So where does that leave mainstream journalists personally sympathetic to the Palestinian cause? Presenting the actual Palestinian point of view—documenting the daily reality of life under military occupation, explaining how the Israeli army broke the 2008 ceasefire, or, god forbid, talking about a genuine "national liberation struggle"—is simply "too dangerous" for their careers. So, in place of this, journalists showed what one called an "endless procession of grief". This effectively served as a proxy in place of the "Palestinian side of the argument" that was simply not allowed an airing. In other words, during the Gaza massacre of 2008-2009, viewers were treated to pictures of Palestinian suffering—but the *analysis* was consistently pro-Israeli, emphasising the themes favoured by their spokesmen (rocket fire, the obligation to protect its citizens, Hamas breaking the ceasefire, etc). As a result, the focus groups used in Philo's research, whilst horrified by the tragedy of the Palestinian situation, dutifully trotted out the Israeli propaganda that had been their staple diet from the news coverage—that the Palestinians had brought it all on themselves.

Again, this seems to be true of the war on Libya—but this time, it is not only true of the mainstream media, but a substantial portion of the "radical" media and intelligentsia as well. Once the bombing is well underway, the liberal left—who had been either applauding or silent about the outbreak of the pro-NATO contra rebellion—were happy enough condemning the resulting atrocities. But the analysis (albeit often implicit on the left) remains—as with Palestine—that the pro-Gaddafi forces had "brought it on themselves" by being intolerably repressive, or using violence on peaceful protesters, etc, etc. Where is the actual *analysis* from the other point of view? Where is the explanation of the serious material and financial contribution that Gaddafi was making to African unity, or to keeping the continent free of U.S. bases? Where are the comments pointing out that *all 700* imprisoned members of the Libyan Islamic Fighting Group involved in previous violent uprisings against the Libyan state had been freed in a process of reconciliation in the eighteen months preceding the rebellion—the last batch being released even as the early stages of the uprising was already underway? Where were the voices explaining that the neo-liberal credentials of all leading NTC members would surely sign the death knell for Libya's four decades history of generous social provision, that had resulted in the highest life expectancy on the continent?

Cameron has said the Libya intervention was the "model" for the coming colonial wars (he called them humanitarian interventions of course). Knowing this, radical media has a duty to learn the lessons. Will we be fooled into supporting contra rebellions in Syria, Iran, Algeria, China, too? Or will we reject the media's duty to "keep people ignorant" and defend the sovereignty of independent nations threatened by imperial aggression? ☐

The Dark Knight Rises

A masterpiece of white supremacist fantasy

GOTHAM City is taken hostage by a gang of vicious terrorists. They have crawled out of a dark hole in the Middle East, and one has even managed to pass herself off as a Gothamite. They have made common cause with 1000 Gotham prisoners in orange jumpsuits. They have managed to get hold of a device for creating nuclear power—but the wily swine have found a way to turn it into a nuclear bomb. Their crazed fanaticism means that their only use for technology is as a means of genocide. They are led by a man called Bane. His face is covered. He is a psychopath.

It doesn't take much decoding to work out what all this represents. It is a powerful piece of propaganda in the war against Iran. But it also taps into a much older story that white people have been telling themselves for years—the fear of being swamped by the black masses. If they are ever allowed to crawl out of their dark hole, the story goes, this is what happens. They will get into our societies. They will mix with us. Then they will destroy us.

Of course, these fears disguise the fact that it is precisely *us*, the white nations, which *already* do these things the world over. The film's scenes of violent criminals being let out of prison and armed, of summary justice in mock courts, of public lynchings: this is what has just been imposed by NATO on Libya. The killing of scientists, the constant threat of all out war, the blockade of the city to intimidate the population: this is what the Europe and America are doing to Iran *today*. The random bomb attacks, the war against the police, the co-option of sections of the army under threat of total destruction: this is precisely the reality of the West's proxy war against Syria.

It is a psychological truism that what we hate most in others is what we refuse to see about ourselves. We kid ourselves that our own

Films like The Dark Knight prey on racist fear and prejudice.

hatred and brutality is actually an attribute of our victims: and thus justify their destruction. We imagine they are as bad as us.

What makes us so convinced—without even five minutes serious study or thought on the issue—that Gaddafi, or Assad, or Ahmadinejad is a bloodthirsty murderous tyrant? We don't feel the need to look into specifics—because we know their *type*. We have grown up with these archetypal evil figures—we know them from the movies and stories we've been telling each other our whole lives. We know exactly what *these people* are like. What we don't necessarily want to accept is that these archetypes are actually based on *ourselves*. However successful we may be at keeping the fact out of our conscious minds, we know, in our hearts, what genocidal depravities underpin, and have always underpinned, Western/white supremacy in the world. Our most honoured national figures[1] are open supporters of genocide.[2] We know *we* are bloodthirsty murderous tyrants. But the stories we tell our children—stories such as the Dark Knight Rises—allow us to project these qualities onto our enemies. When we wage war, it is not against "Gaddafi", but the *imagined* Gaddafi, the one we know very well—because the imagined Gaddafi is *us*.

The battle ends with scenes of euphoria as the jubilant Gothamites cheer on a mushroom cloud from a nuclear bomb dropped over the sea (overseas?). Of course, in the film, no one actually dies in this explosion—but isn't that exactly what we tell ourselves about our

wars anyway? No one really dies at our hands—no one of any consequence anyway—only demons, Gaddafi-ites, insurgents; sub-humans.
Won't the war against Iran just involve a 'surgical strike' against
'facilities'? We will be able to find a way to applaud the overseas
mushroom cloud, one way or another; after all, we will say—it's no
worse than what they would do to us. Don't you know what these
people are like? Haven't you *seen* Batman? ☐

Part Seven
Resistance at Home

Wealth redistribution and police accountability

Why are we leaving it to our children?

RIOTING and looting was not the only violent activity being carried out by Englishmen on Sunday night. Some hours before Cameron appeared on our TV screens vowing to take revenge on the risen British youth, his bomber pilots carried out a raid which reportedly slaughtered 33 Libyan children, along with 32 women and 20 men in Zlitan, a village near Tripoli. He, along with the rulers of France and the U.S., are desperately trying to stave off economic collapse in the same way they always have—through the slaughter of third world people and the theft of their resources.

That is the context in which these riots need to be seen. Our mode of living in the West is predicated on violence and looting. For those who do not understand this, you need to look into how Western military forces have turned Afghanistan into a giant heroin poppy plantation[1] with the lowest life expectancy on the planet outside sub-Saharan Africa;[2] how they have turned Iraq into a living hell[3] to steal its oil,[4] how they are setting up Syria for an invasion as a prelude to the "final solution" of the Palestinian "problem"[5] and how they are already stealing Libyan oil wealth[6] which Gaddafi had ploughed into African development but will now go straight into the coffers of arms companies to buy arms[7] for the racist rebel army.[8] This is before we even mention the debt-extortion under which third world countries pay 13 times as much in loan interest to the West (on loans they have already paid back many times over) than they receive in aid.[9]

Our young people have grown up witnessing all of this. They are well aware that the West enriches itself by violent plunder. They are also aware that more than half of their so-called "representatives" in parliament have been systematically stealing TVs, electronic goods, clothes and anything else they think they can get away with, by means of large-scale fraud.[10] They know that the police murder people with impunity,[11] and their communities are subject to harassment and humiliation by police on a mass scale.[12] They know that the bankers who have destroyed the livelihoods of millions, are still paying themselves bonuses extorted from the public purse.[13]

They also know that none of these people are ever likely to be brought to justice through legal mechanisms. Most of the MPs guilty of fraud either still have their jobs, or have moved on to lucrative directorships with the companies for whom they did favours whilst in office. The police investigate themselves and find themselves not guilty. Army officers investigate themselves and find themselves not guilty. Tony Blair investigates himself and finds himself not guilty. The rich and powerful are demonstrating to our young people daily that the way to succeed is through robbery, theft and violence. This is the world into which they were born. This is the morality which surrounds them. This is the air they breathe.

Compared to their role models, the vast majority of the rioters have behaved impeccably. Attacks on small businesses, houses and civilians have been the exception, not the rule; the main activity has been the looting of big chain stores and the besieging of police stations. In so doing, the youth have succeeded in achieving what everyone else has failed to achieve—holding the police and corporations to account. The message to the police has been clear—you cannot murder, beat and humiliate us with impunity. Several police stations have been torched and all London police have had their summer leave cancelled. When incidents like Mark Duggan's murder arise, it is never a case of one "bad apple"; the process of cover-up is a systematic one which requires large-scale collusion. Some officers may now think twice before getting entangled in such matters in the future.

As for the big corporations, the efficiency of their exploitation and enslavement of third world people has created such poverty across the globe that people are increasingly unable to afford to buy what they produce. This is the major systemic cause of the economic crisis. They may not know it, but the corporations our children are attacking are indeed the major cause of their own poverty. More than this, these companies employ advertising techniques that ruthlessly target our children with a cruel message that their social status depends on the acquisition of their goods; they should not then feign surprise when poor children also try to acquire them.

With their so-called "mindless looting", the dispossessed youth are in fact carrying out a primitive form of wealth redistribution. What they are doing in a disorganised and spontaneous way, is precisely what we *should* be doing in a systematic and disciplined way. We need to build organisations that are serious about creating "socialism from below"—taking control of the factories, chain stores and land, and using them in a way that provides for the massive social needs for which capitalism is completely unable to provide. This is the real Big Society—the one Cameron and his ilk are terrified of.

I am not blaming Cameron, or the politicians, or the media, by the way. These are our enemies. They are being true to their class. They are exploiting us and lying to us efficiently and effectively. They are doing their jobs perfectly. I am blaming those of us who *do* care, who do want equality and an end to classism, racism and imperialism. We need to step up and provide leadership and organisation, and until we do that—our criticisms of the youth are hollow and deceitful. If we leave it to children to bring accountability to policing and to redistribute wealth, without any leadership or guidance, we shouldn't be surprised if they do a messy job. ☐

How David Starkey is right

'The whites are becoming black'

SPEAKING about the London riots last week, David Starkey told Newsnight that the big problem in today's society "is that the chavs...have become black; the whites have become black."

In a sense, he is right. One of the biggest problems for him and his fellow white supremacists*, is indeed the danger that English youth begin to side with the third world liberation struggle, rather than with their own government's colonial aggression. And through the white youth's adoption of black cultural idioms, that process has already begun.

All major forms of popular dance music (from soul and funk to hiphop and jungle) are creations of Africans and their descendants. And, although many of these art forms have subsequently degenerated since coming under the control of giant corporations, at the heart of all of them there was originally a spirit of militant resistance.[1]

One the clearest examples of this is reggae music. Reggae took the iconography of Rastafarianism—perhaps the most accessible and visceral depiction of colonial relations yet articulated—and turned it into a universal language of resistance. Even across the oppressor nations in the West, people fell in love with the beat, and soon began to absorb the message as well. Soon after arriving on these shores, it became a massive inspiration and influence behind the punk movement—another historical moment when "the whites became black"—which briefly appeared as a genuine threat to the class exploitation system.

So black culture *does* tend to embody a spirit of defiance and resistance against the exploiters, their state and its colonial system; white people *are* embracing this culture and it *is* a problem for David Starkey and folks like him.

But there are two sides to the "whites becoming black" coin. Young impoverished whites in England are not only being drawn towards "being black"—they are also being blocked from "being white". To understand this, we need to get to grips with the political purpose behind the concept of "whiteness" in the first place. Theodore Allen has argued convincingly that "whiteness" as a distinct category was invented in the American colonies of Maryland and Virginia in order to prevent property-less Europeans allying with African Americans—by conferring certain privileges onto them. It worked very well—generally speaking, white workers did indeed begin to identify more with their own exploiters than with the Black slaves; the edge was taken off their own exploitation by being granted access to a small share of the more extreme exploitation of the Africans. In the twentieth century a similar process has taken place across Europe through the combination of the welfare state and tough immigration laws. On the one hand, the welfare state for a long time enabled even the most disadvantaged citizens of the "white" countries access to a relatively decent standard of living. On the other, tough immigration laws maintained full employment whilst preventing the vast majority of the *global* workforce any real access to the fruits of their labour. In return, English workers by and large gave their consent to the colonial (and neo-colonial) exploitation that underwrote the whole system.

Today, for property-less whites, those privileges are being obliterated. Since the 1980s, significant sections of "white" society in the West have begun to lose, therefore, the very thing that makes them 'white'—their privileged status. Nell Painter put it clearly in her book The History of White People. For her, whiteness is "a signal of power, prestige, and beauty *to be withheld and granted selectively"*. For the white "underclass" in England, it is a status that is rapidly being withdrawn.

Nowhere is this more clear than in the demonization of the so-called "chav". The middle class stereotype of the "chav" is much like the racist stereotype of the "n****r"—lazy, stupid, violent etc. But in fact it also incorporates the more specific stereotype of the *"uppity* n****r": a member of the underclass who "doesn't know his place"; who gets ideas "above his station"; in other words, who refuses to accept his subordinate position in society. How else can we interpret the endless middle class mockery of the "bling" worn by poor youth? Jewellery *itself* is not condemned—what is being condemned is the right of the poor to wear it.

So, losing their privileged "white" status, being subjected to old, *racist*, stereotypes in a new form, and attracted to the oppositional pride and defiance of black music and culture, white youth in poor areas *are* ceasing to be "white" and are instead "becoming black". On a cultural level, they are joining the "fourth world"—those in the West with ancestral homelands in the third world, who by and large constitute the dispossessed of the West, and as such form the most potentially revolutionary class.

This all came to a head in the riots last week, where poor white youth joined with black people in what was originally an outburst of anger against brutal and *racist* policing.[2] The fact that many then subsequently took the opportunity to stock up on the goods they have been denied, or even that some went on to commit arson or murder, should not detract from this fact.**

So we should perhaps be thanking Starkey for bringing the issue of race into the debate from where it had been conspicuously absent hitherto. But the real problem—from our perspective—is not that the "whites think they're black". Inasmuch as "white" is a symbol of privilege and the "right to rule", the real problem is that people like David Starkey think they're "white". ☐

*By white supremacist, I mean here those who favour the continued domination of the globe by the European and European settler nations (the so-called 'first world').

**It is important to remember that gang violence and burglary were not something new, brought about by the riots—they were already taking place before the riots; in fact, gang violence may actually may have decreased during the riots.[3]

With thanks to Sukant Chandan and Dr Lez Henry for encouraging me to think about these things...not that either of them necessarily agree with my views!

Another innocent man persecuted by British police

Perry Atherton: political prisoner

An edited version of this article was originally published by the Morning Star, November 14 2012

LAST July, the future looked bright for Perry Atherton: twenty-two years old, he had a good job and had just moved into his own flat in Nottingham's desirable Mapperley neighbourhood. Today all that is gone, as he enters the fourth month of a three-year sentence for violent disorder. He is one of many victims of the political crackdown that followed the youth uprisings in urban centres across England last August; yet unlike most, he was not even involved in those uprisings. Convicted, as his mother says, of being "in the wrong place at the wrong time", Perry was framed for a crime he didn't commit by a racist police force desperate to produce results for a government demanding convictions.

On the evening of Tuesday 9 August 2011, Perry Atherton had gone out to buy some food from the local shops in Mansfield Rd, near his mother's home in Nottingham. When he arrived, he noticed a police helicopter circling overhead, and a number of police in the area. The disturbances following the execution of Mark Duggan had spread to Nottingham the day before, and a group of youths had just climbed onto the roof of the nearby school. A number of people had come out into the street in the same area as Perry, watching the helicopter and wondering what was going on. Perry decided to go round the corner to investigate. A small group of youths were milling around, and smoke was rising from a nearby bin that had been set on fire. The next minute, three police vans screeched round the corner, and twenty police officers charged out of the vans. Everyone started to run—including Perry—but the police caught him and knocked him to the ground, whereupon they racially abused him and arrested him.

The police tell the story rather differently. The jury in Nottingham crown court were told that there was a riot in Mansfield Road that evening, and that Perry had set a bin on fire and then thrown a petrol bomb at the police.

Despite being assigned a different defence solicitor for each hearing—each of whom invariably knew few of the details of the case—the initial court hearings seemed to be going in Perry's favour.

Despite being assigned a different defence solicitor for each hearing—each of whom invariably knew few of the details of the case—the initial court hearings seemed to be going in Perry's favour. The judge at Nottingham magistrate's court even ordered Perry's tag to be removed as the total absence of any convincing evidence against him became increasingly clear. At one point, the judge, Tim Devas, seemed to lose all patience and demanded to know whether the prosecution actually had anything at all to connect the accused to the events of that night. Something was mumbled about more time being needed to gather evidence, and that they were awaiting results of various tests.

When the results of the tests came back, however, they too put Perry in the clear. His clothes had been sent off to be checked for traces of petrol or debris, but none were found. Phone records had been obtained in an attempt to prove Perry's association with known gang members, but this likewise revealed nothing. CCTV footage showed Perry engaged in nothing more sinister than walking down Mansfield Road.

The only real evidence against Perry consisted of statements made by PC Cattel and PC Walker, the two arresting officers, that Perry had thrown a petrol bomb at the police and set fire to a bin. Whilst they themselves had not actually been there at the time, they claimed that two other officers, Leonardi and Craner, had witnessed it all and identified Perry as the perpetrator. They informed the detaining sergeant of all this just before the twenty-four limit for detention without charge was reached and Perry would have to have been released. Up until that point, the detaining sergeant had noted in his log of Perry's arrest—"No evidence to charge".

The strange thing is that if Leonardi and Craner had witnessed this criminal behaviour, neither of them chose to mention it in their original statements at the time. On the contrary, they claimed that whilst missiles had been thrown at the police, they could not identify either what was thrown, or who threw them. It was only months later that the identity of the thrower suddenly revealed itself to them, and that they suddenly remembered that those unidentifiable missiles were in fact petrol bombs.

More evidence was to come. According to the prosecution, a JD sports bag containing rocks, rubble and traces of petrol was found next to Perry and one of his two co-defendants. But the same bag was also recorded by police as having been found several streets away next to the third co-defendant. This discrepancy did not come out in court, and was only discovered afterwards by Perry's mother Kathleen Atherton as she scoured the arrest sheets that the multiple hurried defence lawyers had clearly not had the time to look at.

There were other discrepancies in the prosecution case. The incident for which Perry was supposedly arrested—the disturbances where police were attacked—occurred, according to the official police log from the day, at 8.50 p.m.—five minutes *after* the time of Perry's arrest recorded on the arrest sheets.

So a handful of police statements, many of which contradicted earlier statements made by the same people, and a bag that was in two places at the same time, constituted the entirety of the substantive evidence against Perry. Other than that, the prosecution case seems to have amounted to comments about his clothing and his bandana which apparently demonstrated that he was "dressed for battle". ("If that's dressed for battle, I'm dressed for battle every day of my life" Perry commented), along with unfounded insinuations about "gang membership". The fact that there were always three people on trial together—one of whom had a number of prior convictions and actually "appeared" in court via satellite link from his holding cell—also added to the overall impression of criminality. As Kathleen Atherton commented, "the jury based their decision on false information from the prosecution, excessive negative media coverage and defamation of character. Officers' falsely accused him of 'gang affiliation' and sought, by placing him alongside the two others, firstly to secure and guarantee the charge, and also to accentuate and dramatise the whole situation."

The hostile media coverage Perry's mother refers to, combined with venomous attacks from government on the "rioters", undoubtedly led to an atmosphere of immense pressure to convict and to punish. The Prime Minister himself called for the imprisonment of every "rioter" (however defined), and the government issued instructions to magistrates' clerks to disregard sentencing guidelines so that they could do exactly that. The result is that those young people (one in three of whom had never been convicted of anything before) that took part in last year's uprisings have been jailed for 4.5 times the average sentence for the crime committed—as a direct result of political interference. In a country whose sense of superiority is based in large part on its supposed respect for the "rule of law" and judicial independence—and which even justifies wars of obliteration against other states on this basis—it took surprisingly little for the whole concept to be tossed out of the window.

What the case of Perry Atherton shows, however, is that it was not only those "caught up" in the riots who became the victims of this process. Even those who had nothing to do with it have had their lives devastated, in order to "set an example" to others. This is politically-motivated collective punishment of innocents; the very opposite of the "rule of law" Britain claims to hold so dear. It should be exposed and condemned—and Perry Atherton should be freed and his record cleared. □

Endnotes

Chapter Five: The West aims to turn the entire global South into a failed state

1   http://www.guardian.co.uk/business/2011/jul/28/centrica-british-gas-profits-refuel-row-over-prices

2   http://www.dailymail.co.uk/news/article-1332343/Nine-pensioners-died-cold-hour-winter-prices-soar.html

3   http://www.thirdworldtraveler.com/Globalization/Globalization_GuideTo.html

4   http://www.who.int/trade/glossary/story084/en/index.html

5   http://www.guardian.co.uk/commentisfree/2008/apr/15/amanmadefamine

6   http://www.oecd.org/dataoecd/25/14/35274754.pdf

7   http://www.youtube.com/watch?v = XhJDGVWtMPA&feature = mfu_in_order&list = UL

8   http://www.non-gmoreport.com/articles/jun08/countries_starve_while_agribusiness_profits.php

9   http://www.telegraph.co.uk/health/healthnews/8747701/NHS-reforms-present-huge-opportunities-for-private-companies-says-minister.html

10 http://blogs.ft.com/westminster/2011/04/elderly-bear-the-brunt-of-council-cuts/#axzz1ejuqIgdz

11 http://feraljundi.com/1338/industry-talk-good-year-for-private-security-by-jody-ray-bennett/

12 http://www.telegraph.co.uk/finance/economics/8901828/Jim-ONeill-China-could-overtake-US-economy-by-2027.html

13 http://www.guardian.co.uk/business/2011/aug/23/g4s-eyes-opportunities-in-new-libya

14 http://knizky.mahdi.cz/50_Jeremy_Scahill___Blackwater_The_
    Rise_of_the_Worlds_Most_Powerful_Mercenary_Army.pdf
15 http://weekly.ahram.org.eg/1998/380/op2.htm
16 http://news.change.org/stories/bangladesh-increases-mini-
    mum-wage-despite-walmarts-obstruction
17 http://www.nytimes.com/2009/01/31/business/econo-
    my/31econ.html
18 http://www.independent.co.uk/opinion/commentators/pat-
    rick-cockburn-fragile-iraq-threatened-by-the-return-of-civil-
    war-6272037.html
19 http://www.globalresearch.ca/index.php?context = va&aid = 972
20 http://www.intifada-palestine.com/2011/07/the-big-picture-war-
    on-libya-is-war-on-entire-africa/
21 http://www.ft.com/cms/s/0/7b433662-5ee0-11e0-a2d7-00144fea-
    b49a.html#axzz1frdi7fwd
22 http://rebelgriot.blogspot.com/2011/09/mustafa-ab-
    dul-jalil-and-mahmoud-jibril.html
23 http://www.haaretz.com/news/middle-east/libya-s-tnc-says-for-
    eign-allies-have-priority-for-deals-1.384677
24 http://www.youtube.com/watch?v = Ha1rEhovONU
25 http://www.maltastar.com/pages/r1/ms10dart.asp?a = 17659
26 http://www.thirdworldtraveler.com/Africa/US_Recolonization_
    Congo.html
27 http://www.gata.org/node/5651

Chapter Six: Britain and the Arab Spring

1   http://www.dailymail.co.uk/news/article-2126653/Diamond-
    Jubilee-Queen-invites-ruler-Bahrains-bloody-regime-Windsor-
    Castle-lunch.html
2   http://www.powerbase.info/index.php/Mark_Allen
3   http://www.morningstaronline.co.uk/index.php/content/view/
    full/115181
4   http://www.israelnationalnews.com/News/News.aspx/143026#.
    TskW71aGiSo
5   http://mrzine.monthlyreview.org/2011/forte200411.html
6   http://www.presstv.ir/detail/2012/07/24/252549/syrian-armed-
    rebels-trained-by-uk/

7 http://www.prisonplanet.com/mi6-sas-working-together-to-take-control-in-libya.html
8 http://www.sott.net/articles/show/242637-Wikileaks-U.S.-led-NATO-Troops-Operate-Inside-Syria
9 http://www.islammemo.cc/akhbar/Africa-we-Europe/2010/03/02/95914.html?lang = en-us:
10 http://www.bi-me.com/main.php?c = 3&cg = 3&t = 1&id = 24646
11 http://english.khabaronline.ir/detail/182398/Iran-Islamic-Republic-of-Iran%E2%80%99s-Constitution-Noroozpour-egypt-morsi-Israel-/Politics/Politics
12 http://www.tigraionline.com/un-report-on-somalia.html
13 http://www.guardian.co.uk/world/2007/jun/26/usa.topstories3

Chapter Seven: A war against African development
1 http://www.socialismtoday.org/33/slavery33.html
2 http://econ.lse.ac.uk/ ~ dquah/p/2010.05-Shifting_Distribution_GEA-DQ.pdf
3 http://edition.cnn.com/2011/BU.S.INESS/04/26/us.china.economy/index.html
4 http://www.ligali.org/article.php?id = 1790
5 http://www.au.int/en/organs/fi
6 http://www.globalissues.org/article/3/structural-adjustment-a-major-cause-of-poverty
7 http://zcommunications.org/victims-of-a-civil-war-black-africans-in-libya-by-michael-mcgehee
8 http://www.finalcall.com/artman/publish/World_News_3/article_7886.shtml
9 http://www.southerntimesafrica.com/article.php?title = Why_the_West_wants_Gaddafi_out__&id = 6159

Chapter Eight: The West's war on African development continues
1 http://www.pambazuka.org/en/category/features/81150
2 http://www.telegraph.co.uk/news/worldnews/africaandindian-ocean/democraticrepublicofcongo/9398748/Britain-accused-of-failing-to-speak-out-against-Congo-violence.html
3 http://www.fairtrade.org.uk/includes/documents/cm_docs/2011/C/Cocoa Briefing FINAL 8Sept11.pdf
4 http://www.gata.org/node/5651/print

5 http://allafrica.com/stories/201104150792.html
6 http://www.realclearworld.com/2009/12/10/africa_getting_a_good_deal_from_china_106976.html
7 http://www.bloomberg.com/apps/news?pid = newsarchive&sid = acXcm.yk56Ko
8 http://allafrica.com/stories/201207131248.html
9 http://www.counterpunch.org/2011/07/27/lies-of-the-libyan-war/
10 http://english.alarabiya.net/articles/2012/01/17/188838.html
11 http://www.thabombekifoundation.org.za/Pages/Dullah-Omar-Eighth-Memorial-Lecture-By-The-Tmf-Patron.aspx
12 http://www.guardian.co.uk/world/2012/jul/13/islamists-mali-threat-europe
13 http://www.jamestown.org/single/?no_cache = 1&tx_ttnews%5btt_news%5d = 40367&tx_ttnews%5bback-Pid%5d = 381&cHash = 5a7b4cffa91bea02b8d8f33718a6656d
14 http://www.independent.co.uk/news/world/africa/algeria-hostage-crisis-grim-news-that-can-be-traced-to-the-triumphant-removal-of-gaddafi-8456521.html
15 http://www.ft.com/cms/s/0/27183132-c8d2-11de-8f9d-00144feabdc0.html#axzz2KPW9O6Bw
16 http://www.cnbc.com/id/100296208/Algeria_a_convert_to_OPEC_price_hardliner_camp
17 http://www.naturalgaseurope.com/strategic-importance-of-algerian-natural-gas-for-europe
18 http://www.telegraph.co.uk/news/worldnews/africaandindianocean/mali/9814559/France-aims-for-total-reconquest-of-Mali.html
19 http://www.proxsa.org/resources/9-11/Brzezinski-980115-interview.htm
20 http://www.reuters.com/article/2012/10/29/us-algeria-usa-mali-idUSBRE89S0UC20121029
21 http://www.bbc.co.uk/news/world-europe-20795750

Chapter Nine: Strategic alignment or a safe pair of hands?
1 http://www.reuters.com/article/2012/06/14/us-syria-crisis-contact-idUSBRE85D0QV20120614

Chapter Ten: NATO has been cultivating its Libyan allies since 2007
1 http://english.aljazeera.net/news/africa/2011/02/20112167051422444.html
2 http://www.bloomberg.com/news/2011-03-21/libyan-rebel-council-sets-up-oil-company-to-replace-qaddafi-s.html
3 http://cablesearch.org/cable/view.php?id = 09TRIPOLI955&hl = benotman
4 http://www.bbc.co.uk/news/world-africa-14613679
5 http://wikileaks.org/cable/2010/01/10TRIPOLI78.html
6 http://wikileaks.org/cable/2010/01/10TRIPOLI78.html
7 http://46.4.48.8/cablegate/wire.php?id = 09TRIPOLI386&search = jibril National Economic Development Board
8 http://cablesearch.org/cable/view.php?id = 09TRIPOLI955&hl = benotman
9 http://www.dailymail.co.uk/debate/article-2034059/Sir-Mark-Allen-The-spy-quit-MI6-BPs-oil-cash--set-train-Labours-love-tyrant-Gaddafi.html
10 http://www.dailymail.co.uk/debate/article-2034059/Sir-Mark-Allen-The-spy-quit-MI6-BPs-oil-cash--set-train-Labours-love-tyrant-Gaddafi.html

Chapter Eleven: An ongoing disaster
1 http://www.guardian.co.uk/world/2012/mar/31/libya-tribal-clashes-sabha-deaths
2 http://www.bbc.co.uk/news/world-africa-17995427
3 http://www.newsdaily.com/stories/bre8491ed-us-libya-minister/
4 http://www.workers.org/2012/world/libya_0524/
5 http://af.reuters.com/article/worldNews/idAFTRE-7AN1W820111124
6 http://www.nytimes.com/2011/08/25/world/africa/25assess.html?pagewanted = all
7 http://www.africom.mil/getArticle.asp?art = 7673
8 http://blogs.shu.edu/diplomacy/2011/12/the-african-union-after-gaddafi/
9 http://www.africanews.it/english/kadhafi%E2%80%99s-africa-the-untold-story-by-j-p-pougala/

Chapter Twelve: The imperial agenda of the US's 'Africa Command'
marches on
1   http://www.guardian.co.uk/news/datablog/2009/sep/17/
    afghanistan-casualties-dead-wounded-british-data
2   http://www.foreignpolicy.com/articles/2010/07/21/the_truth_
    about_africom?page = 0,0
3   http://www.foreignpolicy.com/articles/2010/07/21/the_truth_
    about_africom
4   http://www.foreignaffairs.com/articles/67844/jonathan-steven-
    son/africoms-libyan-expedition
5   http://news.bbc.co.uk/1/hi/7868828.stm
6   http://blogs.shu.edu/diplomacy/2011/12/the-african-union-af-
    ter-gaddafi/
7   http://www.guardian.co.uk/world/2011/oct/14/obama-sends-
    troops-uganda
8   http://www.washingtonpost.com/world/national-security/
    us-trains-african-soldiers-for-somalia-mission/2012/05/13/gIQA-
    JhsPNU_story.html
9   http://www.guardian.co.uk/world/2012/jan/21/somalia-fight-
    ing-mogadishu-african-union
10 http://allafrica.com/stories/201204090676.html
11 http://www.washingtonpost.com/opinions/libyas-path-ahead-is-
    unclear-as-elections-loom/2012/05/22/gIQAULiWiU_story.html
12 http://blogs.shu.edu/diplomacy/2011/12/the-african-union-af-
    ter-gaddafi/

Chapter Fourteen: When are humans not human?
1   http://video.google.com/videoplay?do-
    cid = -6241513179213272889
2   http://www.telegraph.co.uk/news/worldnews/africaandindian-
    ocean/libya/8498817/Libya-Osama-bin-Ladens-death-is-warning-
    to-Gaddafi.html
3   http://www.guardian.co.uk/world/2012/mar/28/left-to-die-mi-
    grants-boat-inquiry
4   http://www.amnesty.org/en/library/info/MDE19/025/2011/en
5   http://www.bbc.co.uk/news/10450556
6   http://rt.com/business/news/libya-war-economy-losses-295/

7   http://www.breakingnews.ie/world/nato-must-bomb-libya-infra-structure-says-uk-general-505101.html

8   http://news.yahoo.com/nato-bombs-libyan-state-tv-transmit-ters-075048584.html

9   http://english.pravda.ru/news/world/23-07-2011/118577-na-to_war_crimes-0/

10 http://www.eliteukforces.info/uk-military-news/0501012-brit-ish-special-forces-syria.php

11 http://www.bbc.co.uk/news/world-us-canada-19102374

12 http://www.news.com.au/breaking-news/world/syrian-reb-els-accused-of-atrocities/story-e6frfkui-1226442798288

13 http://www.morningstaronline.co.uk/index.php/news/content/view/full/122002

14 http://www.globalresearch.ca/index.php?contex-t = va&aid = 24591

15 http://www.syriahr.com/

16 http://www.bbc.co.uk/news/world-middle-east-18322412

17 http://news.bbc.co.uk/1/hi/uk/6934300.stm

18 http://www.guardian.co.uk/uk/2008/feb/03/afghanistan.iraq

19 http://news.bbc.co.uk/1/hi/uk/6934300.stm

20 http://www.telegraph.co.uk/news/uknews/defence/8732137/RAF-crews-face-sack-as-Libya-campaign-rages.html

21 http://www.bbc.co.uk/news/10450556

Chapter Fifteen: The West's greatest fear is a peaceful resolution

1   http://www.bendbulletin.com/apps/pbcs.dll/arti-cle?AID = /20120423/NEWS0107/204230335/1159&nav_category

Chapter Seventeen: The war on Syria means war on Palestine

1   http://www.bbc.co.uk/news/world-middle-east-20391558

2   http://www.newstatesman.com/politics/2012/11/israel-must-flatten-gaza-us-flattened-japan-says-sharons-son

3   http://app.response.stratfor.com/e/es?s = 1483&e = 611795&elq = d6ccd6477a304cba88d-a55cce8893020

4   http://occidentalisraeli.com/2009/01/06/operation-cast-lead-is-raeli-public/

5   http://www.haaretz.com/news/diplomacy-defense/haaretz-poll-

more-than-90-percent-of-israeli-jews-support-gaza-war.premium-1.478903

6   http://www.middle-east-online.com/english/?id = 51012
7   http://middleeastatemporal.wordpress.com/2012/11/18/hezbollah-remains-wary-amid-israeli-operations-in-gaza/

Chapter Eighteen: The British parliament only likes to attack the weak

1   http://www.reuters.com/article/2012/10/05/us-iran-sanctions-un-idUSBRE89412Z20121005
2   http://english.yonhapnews.co.kr/fullstory/2013/05/30/13/45000
    00000AEN20130530000100315F.HTML
3   http://www.publications.parliament.uk/pa/ld200607/ldselect/
    ldeconaf/96/96i.pdf
4   http://amarillo.com/stories/061801/usn_calliraq.shtml
5   http://www.independent.co.uk/news/uk/crime/british-terror-suspects-quietly-stripped-of-citizenship-then-killed-by-drones-8513858.html
6   http://www.theguardian.com/commentisfree/2013/aug/31/syria-vote-corner-turned
7   http://www.theguardian.com/commentisfree/2013/aug/31/syria-vote-corner-turned
8   http://www.counterpunch.org/2011/07/27/lies-of-the-libyan-war/
9   http://www.theguardian.com/world/2011/mar/12/gaddafi-army-kill-half-million
10 http://www.boston.com/bostonglobe/editorial_opinion/oped/
    articles/2011/04/14/false_pretense_for_war_in_libya/
11 http://www.globalresearch.ca/video-libya-the-humanitarian-war-there-is-no-evidence/27101
12 http://www.independent.co.uk/news/world/africa/gaddafi-defiant-as-protesters-killed-2225667.html
13 http://www.independent.co.uk/news/world/africa/amnesty-questions-claim-that-gaddafi-ordered-rape-as-weapon-of-war-2302037.html
14 http://www.youtube.com/watch?v = IGGbOJYoCGY
15 http://www.independent.co.uk/news/world/africa/amnesty-questions-claim-that-gaddafi-ordered-rape-as-weapon-of-war-2302037.html

16   http://www.independent.co.uk/voices/comment/mps-are-scarred-by-the-war-in-iraq-8792882.html

17   file://localhost/-%2509http/:www.washingtonpost.com:world:national-security:us-military-officers-have-deep-doubts-about-impact-wisdom-of-a-us-strike-on-syria:2013:08:29:825dd5d4-10ee-11e3-b4cb-fd7ce041d814_story.html

18   http://www.stratfor.com/weekly/syria-and-limits-comparison#ixzz2ddxBWbuY

19   http://www.bbc.co.uk/news/world-middle-east-21029034

20   http://www.guardian.co.uk/world/2013/mar/08/west-training-syrian-rebels-jordan

21   http://www.stratfor.com/weekly/obamas-bluff

22   http://www.jamestown.org/regions/middleeast/single/?tx_ttnews%5Btt_news%5D=40491&tx_ttnews%5BbackPid%5D=49&cHash=2d325d815c19548a72bdb22cfea02ead#.UiXmctLVCCc

23   http://www.independent.co.uk/voices/comment/in-syria-its-a-case-of-all-or-nothing-8792975.html

24   http://www.theguardian.com/politics/2013/aug/31/poll-british-military-action-syria

25   http://yougov.co.uk/news/2011/03/22/analysis-opinions-libya/

Chapter Twenty: A masterpiece of white supremacist fantasy

1   http://news.bbc.co.uk/1/hi/entertainment/2509465.stm

2   http://message.snopes.com/showthread.php?t=40602

Chapter Twenty-one: Why are we leaving it to our children?

1   http://www.msnbc.msn.com/id/19431056/ns/world_news-south_and_central_asia/t/un-opium-production-soaring-afghanistan/

2   http://en.wikipedia.org/wiki/List_of_countries_by_life_expectancy

3   http://news.bbc.co.uk/1/hi/5368360.stm

4   http://priceofoil.org/thepriceofoil/war-terror/iraqi-oil-law/

5   http://www.globalresearch.ca/index.php?context=va&aid=24591

6   http://www.msnbc.msn.com/id/41834665/ns/business-world_business/t/treasury-says-billion-libyan-assets-frozen/

7   http://www.bbc.co.uk/news/world-africa-13970412
8   http://tarpley.net/2011/03/30/the-libya-rebels-a-cia-secret-army-of-al-qaeda-terrorists-anti-black-racists-and-monarchists/
9   http://www.un.org/cyberschoolbus/briefing/poverty/poverty.pdf
10 http://news.bbc.co.uk/1/hi/uk_politics/8496729.stm
11 http://www.injusticefilm.co.uk/
12 http://www.telegraph.co.uk/news/uknews/law-and-order/7594021/Huge-rise-in-stop-and-search.html
13 http://www.independent.co.uk/news/uk/politics/back-lash-over-bankers-bonuses-1604034.html

Chapter Twenty-two: 'The whites are becoming black'

1   http://www.zcommunications.org/commerce-is-killing-the-true-spirit-of-hip-hop-by-daveyd
2   http://www.dailymail.co.uk/news/article-1257263/Racist-police-officers-single-black-people-stop-searches.html, http://www.telegraph.co.uk/news/uknews/law-and-order/7594021/Huge-rise-in-stop-and-search.html, http://www.dailymail.co.uk/news/article-2023254/Tottenham-riot-Mark-Duggan-shooting-sparked-police-beating-girl.html
3   http://www.labourlist.org/from-optimist-to-pessimist

CPSIA information can be obtained at www.ICGtesting.com
Printed in the USA
LVOW05s1723020414

380032LV00014B/859/P